Book
Learnin'

Book Learnin'

A Pie Comics Collection

John McNamee

The Arts

ANCIENT ROME

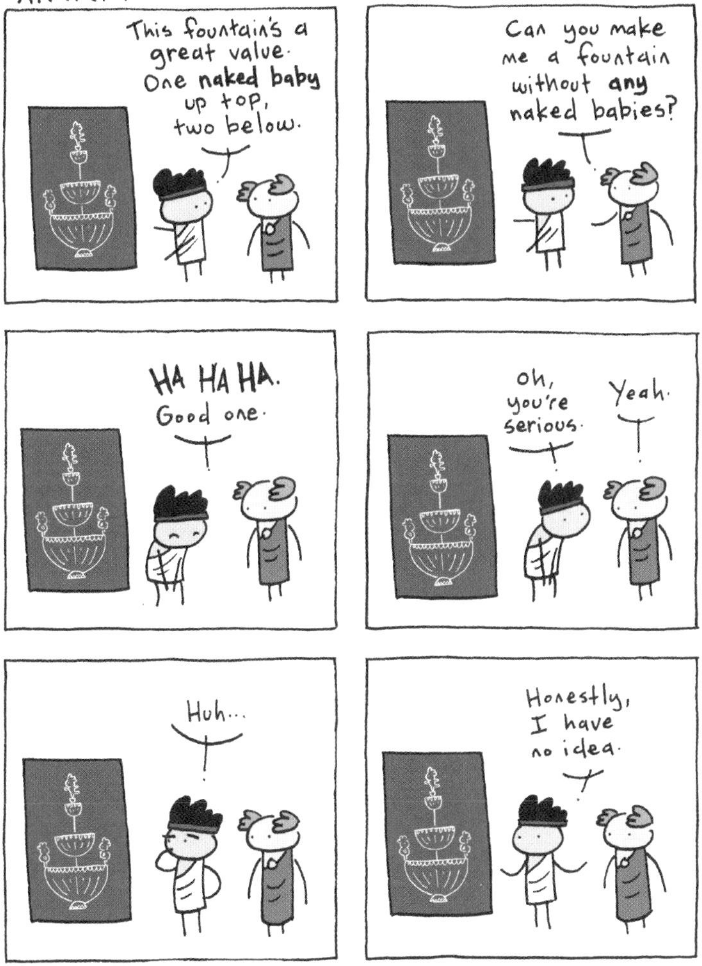

This fountain's a great value. One naked baby up top, two below.
Can you make me a fountain without any naked babies?
HA HA HA. Good one.
Oh, you're serious.
Yeah.
Huh...
Honestly, I have no idea.

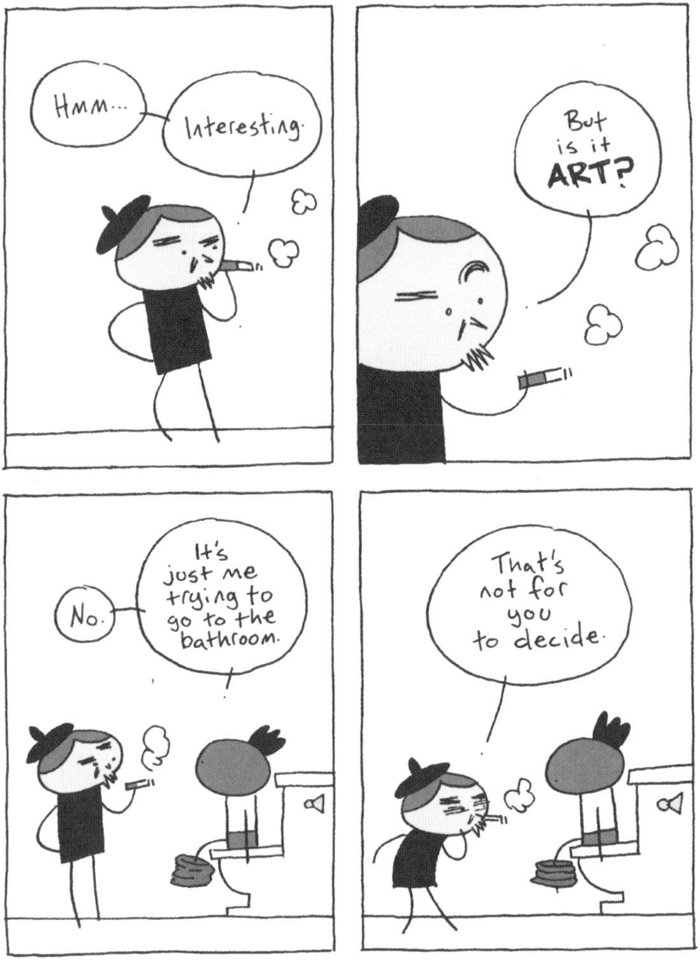
Hmm...
Interesting.
But is it ART?
No.
It's just me trying to go to the bathroom.
That's not for you to decide.

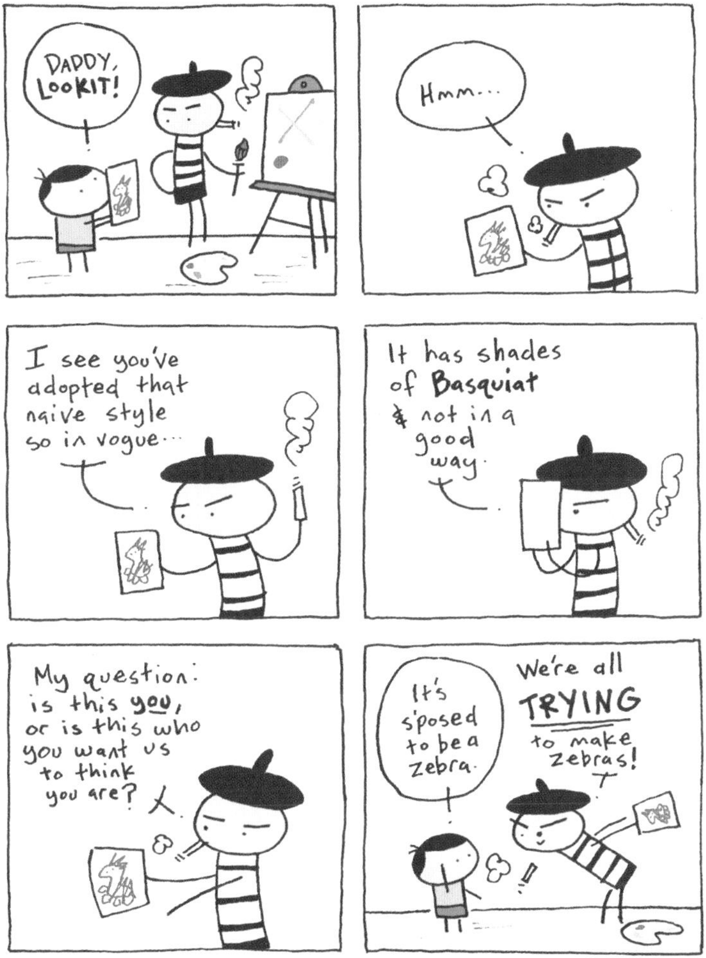
DADDY, LOOKIT!
Hmm...
I see you've adopted that naive style so in vogue...
It has shades of Basquiat & not in a good way.
My question: is this you, or is this who you want us to think you are?
It's s'posed to be a zebra.
We're all TRYING to make zebras!

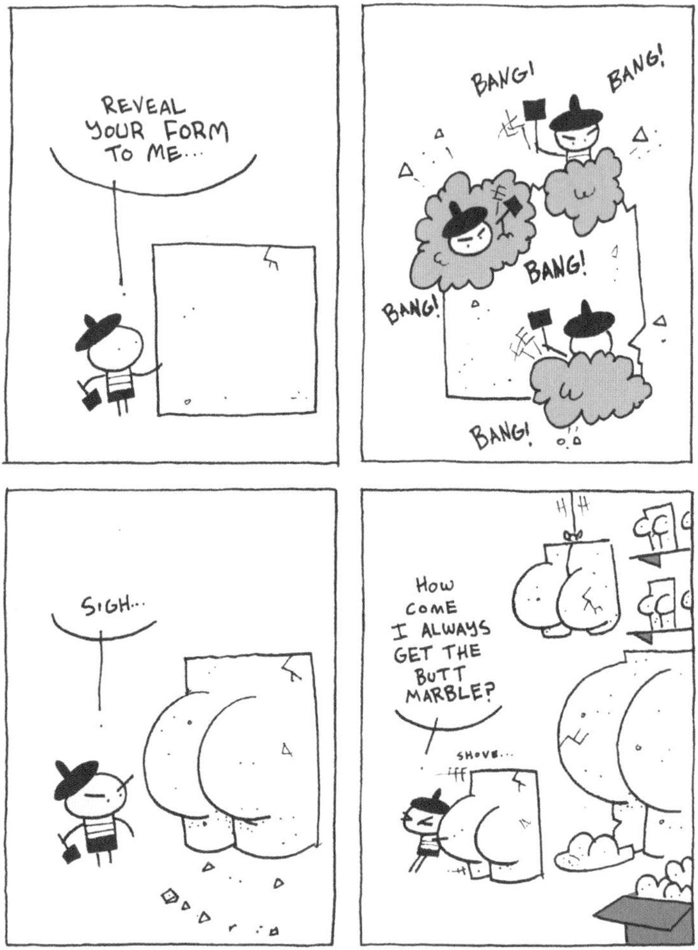
REVEAL YOUR FORM TO ME...
BANG!
BANG!
BANG!
BANG!
BANG!
SIGH...
HOW COME I ALWAYS GET THE BUTT MARBLE?
SHOVE...

ONE DAY MY ART WILL BE APPRECIATED!
Ooooh...
THIS BURNS REAL GOOD!
JUST WISH IT WASN'T SO UGLY.

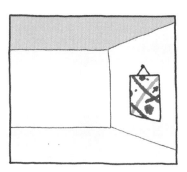

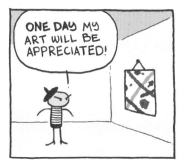

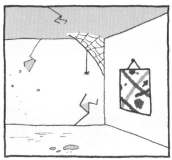

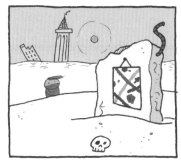

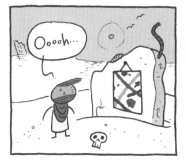

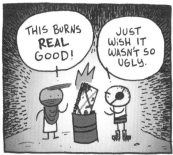

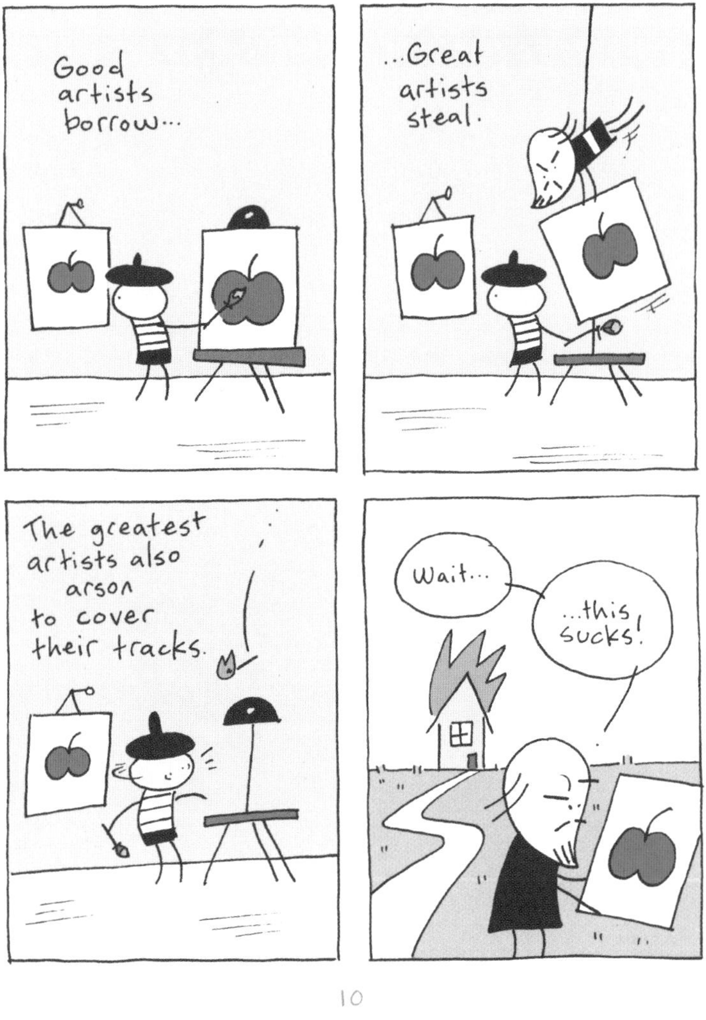
Good artists borrow...
...Great artists steal.
The greatest artists also arson to cover their tracks.
Wait...
...this sucks!

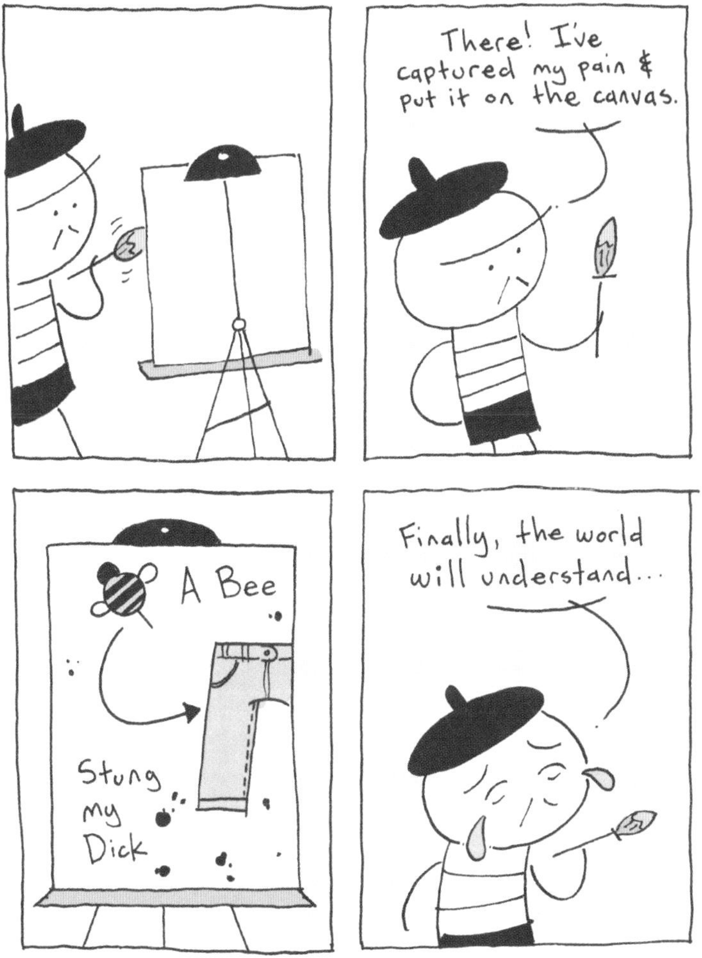
There! I've captured my pain & put it on the canvas.
A Bee
Stung my Dick
Finally, the world will understand...

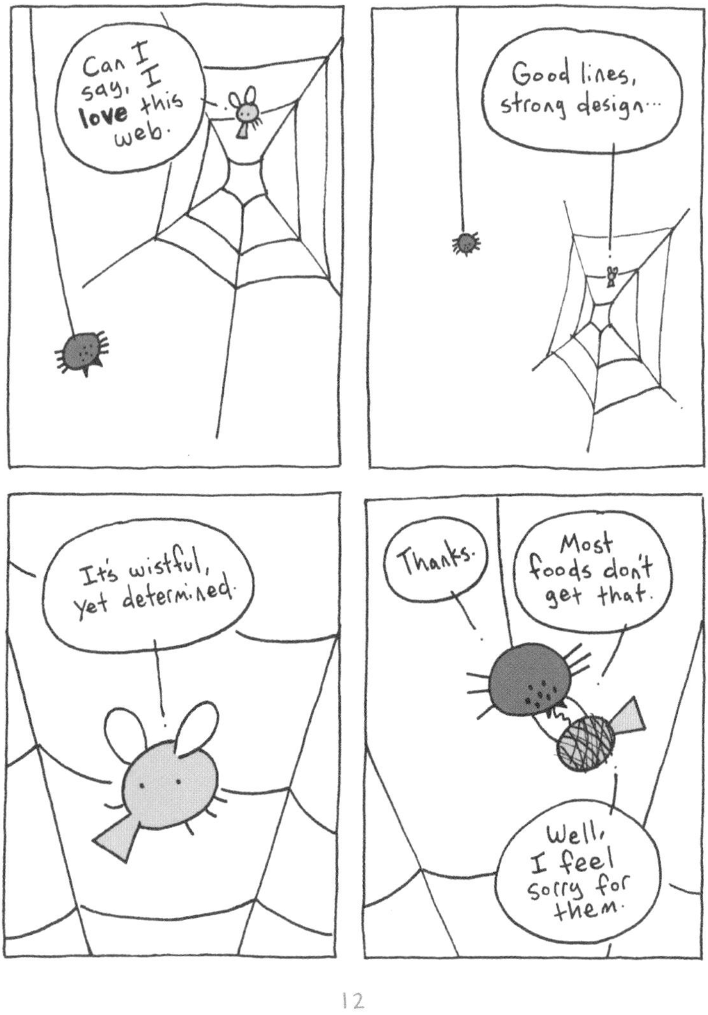
Can I say, I **love** this web.
Good lines, strong design...
It's wistful, yet determined.
Thanks.
Most foods don't get that.
Well, I feel sorry for them.

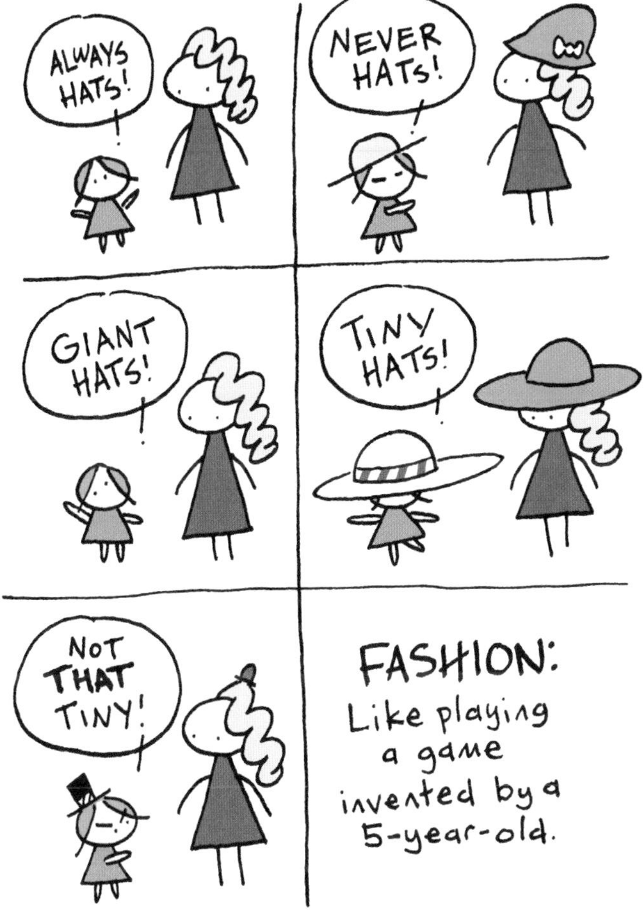
ALWAYS HATS!
NEVER HATS!
GIANT HATS!
TINY HATS!
NOT **THAT** TINY!
FASHION:
Like playing a game invented by a 5-year-old.

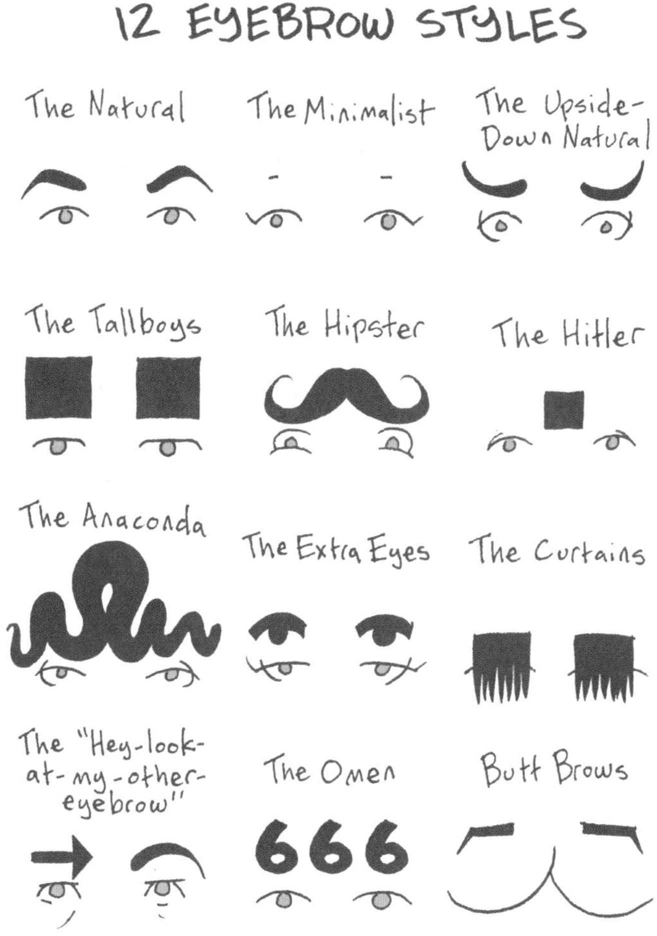
12 EYEBROW STYLES
The Natural
The Minimalist
The Upside-Down Natural
The Tallboys
The Hipster
The Hitler
The Anaconda
The Extra Eyes
The Curtains
The "Hey-look-at-my-other-eyebrow"
The Omen
666
Butt Brows

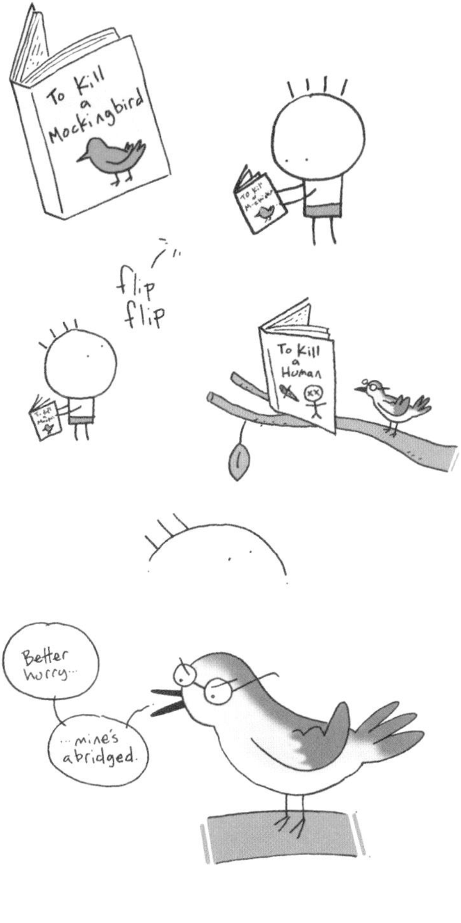
To Kill a Mockingbird
flip
flip
To Kill a Human
Better hurry...
...mine's abridged.

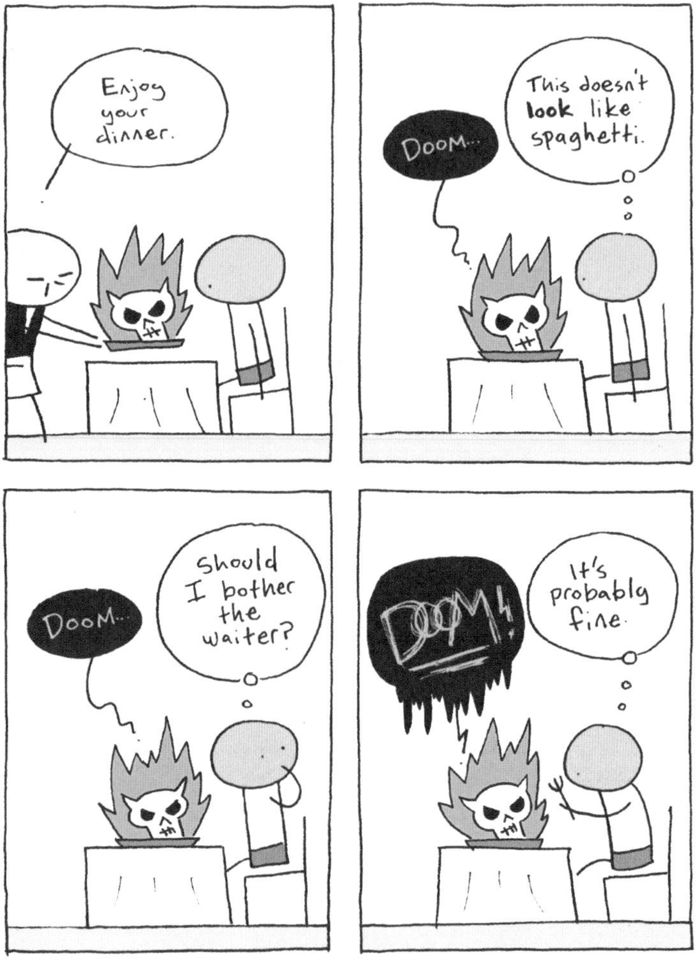
Enjoy your dinner.
DOOM...
This doesn't **look** like spaghetti.
DOOM...
Should I bother the waiter?
DOOM!
It's probably fine.

Dance is the only way I can express my **feelings**.

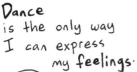

Joy.

Anger.

Wanting to eat a whole block of cheese.

Despair.

Social Sciences

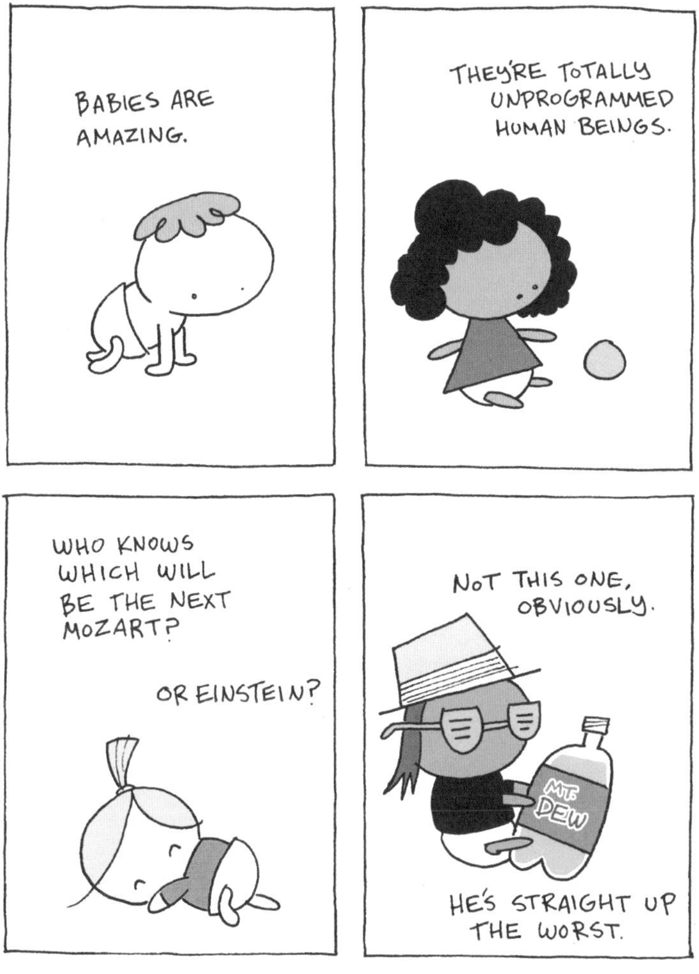
BABIES ARE AMAZING.
THEY'RE TOTALLY UNPROGRAMMED HUMAN BEINGS.
WHO KNOWS WHICH WILL BE THE NEXT MOZART?
OR EINSTEIN?
NOT THIS ONE, OBVIOUSLY.
MT. DEW
HE'S STRAIGHT UP THE WORST.

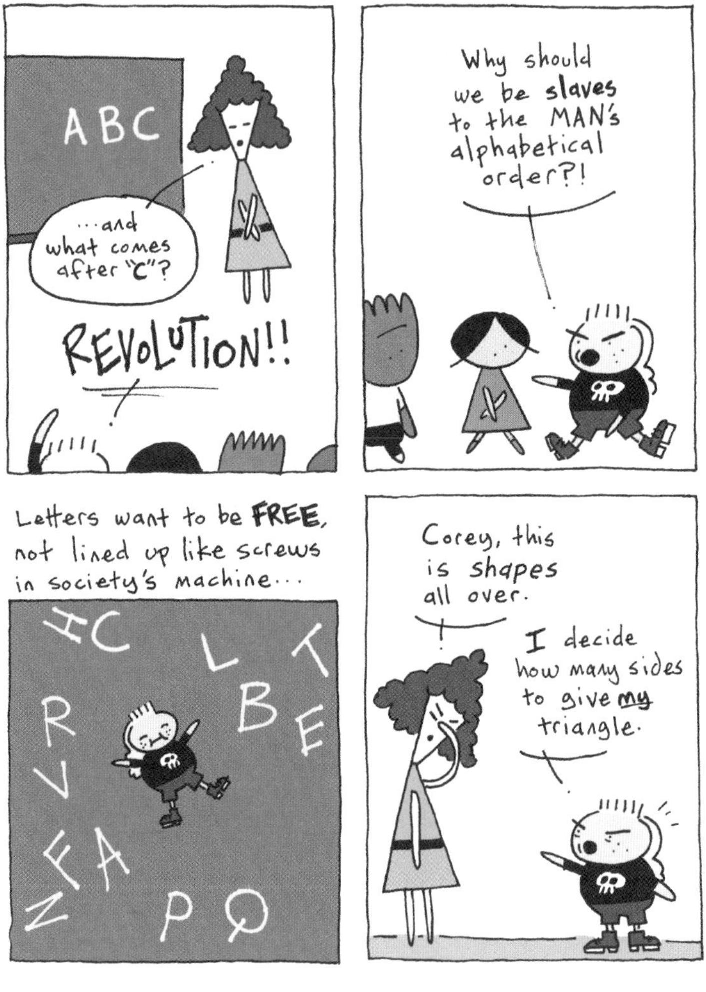
ABC
...and what comes after "C"?
REVOLUTION!!
Why should we be **slaves** to the MAN's alphabetical order?!
Letters want to be **FREE**, not lined up like screws in society's machine...
Corey, this is *shapes* all over.
I decide how many sides to give my triangle.

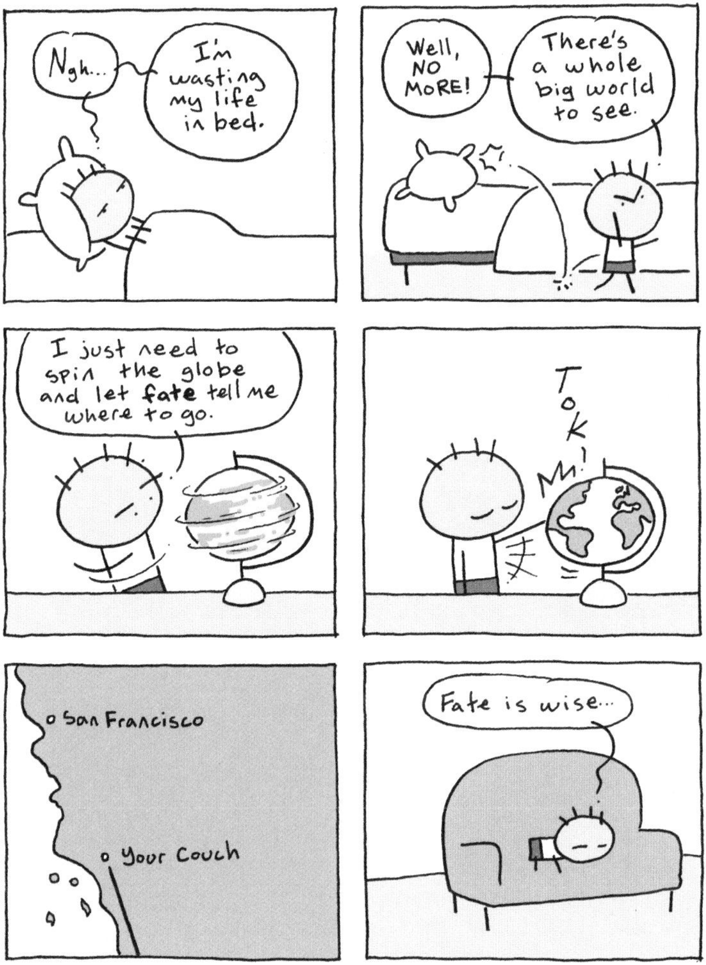
Ngh...
I'm wasting my life in bed.
Well, NO MORE!
There's a whole big world to see.
I just need to spin the globe and let **fate** tell me where to go.
TOK!
Fate is wise...
San Francisco
Your Couch

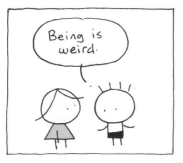

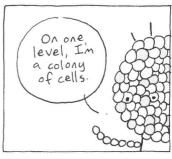

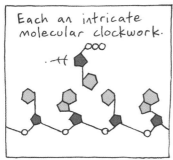

Being is weird.
On one level, I'm a colony of cells.
Each an intricate molecular clockwork.
All of which is just electrons orbiting distant nuclei.
I'm a thin cloud of dust in a sea of emptiness.
A dust governed by its own inscrutable laws.

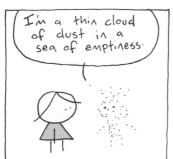

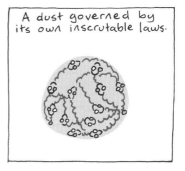

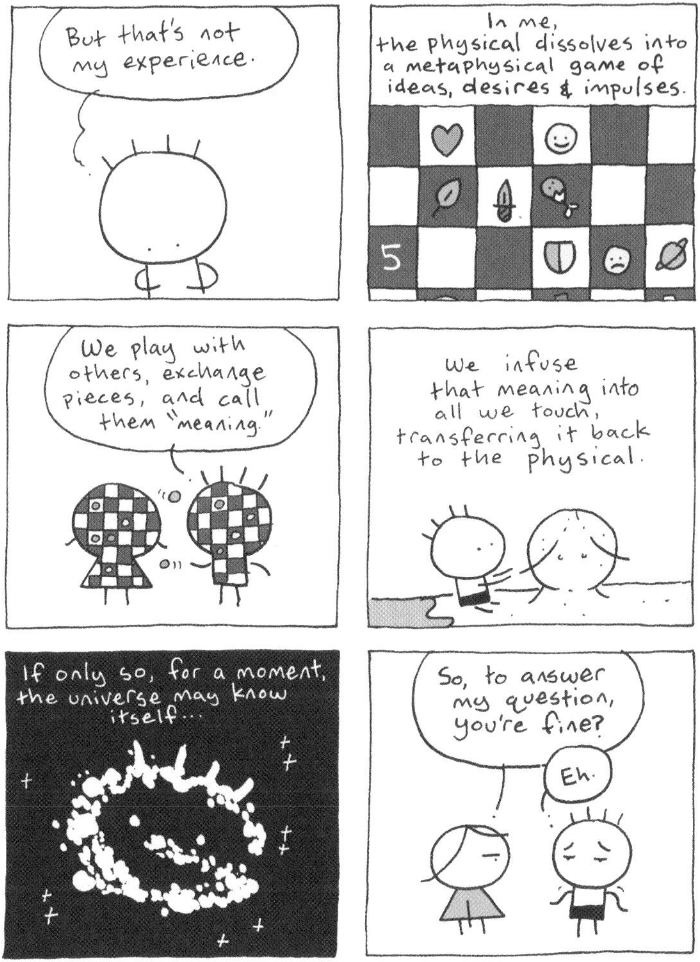
But that's not my experience.
In me, the physical dissolves into a metaphysical game of ideas, desires & impulses.
5
We play with others, exchange pieces, and call them "meaning."
We infuse that meaning into all we touch, transferring it back to the physical.
If only so, for a moment, the universe may know itself...
So, to answer my question, you're fine?
Eh.

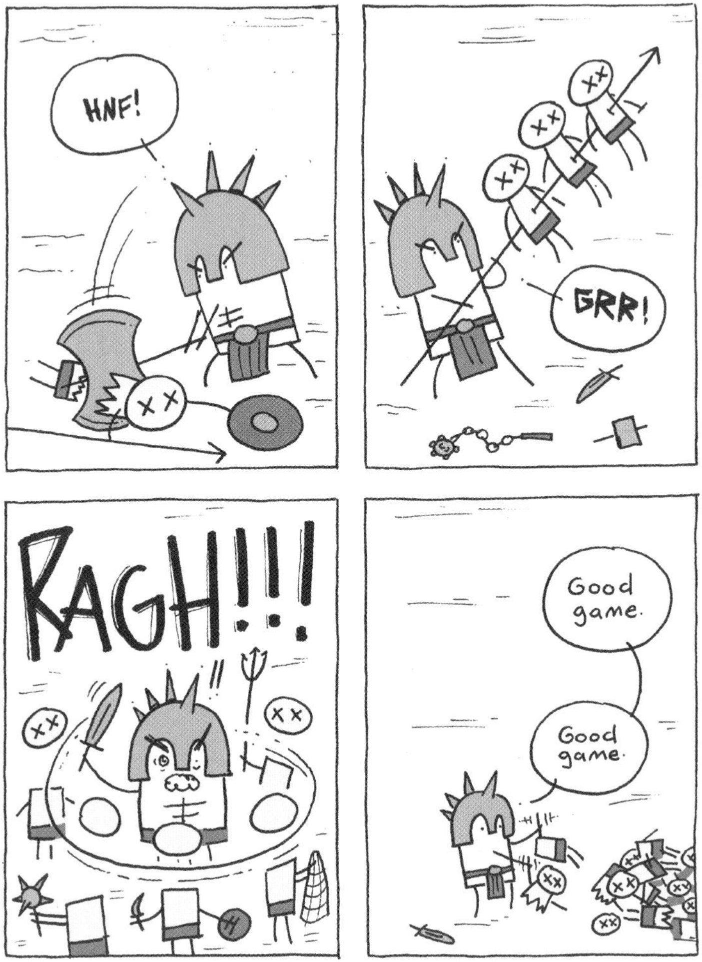
HNF!
GRR!
RAGH!!!
Good game.
Good game.

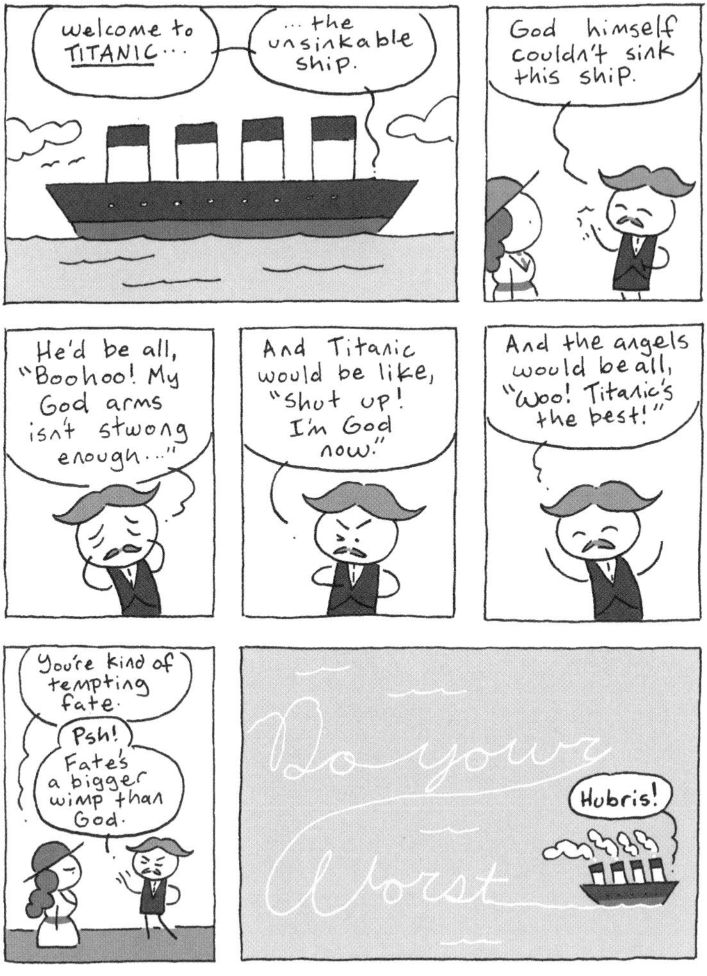
welcome to TITANIC...
...the unsinkable ship.
God himself couldn't sink this ship.
He'd be all, "Boohoo! My God arms isn't stwong enough..."
And Titanic would be like, "Shut up! I'm God now."
And the angels would be all, "Woo! Titanic's the best!"
You're kind of tempting fate.
Psh! Fate's a bigger wimp than God.
Do your Worst
Hubris!

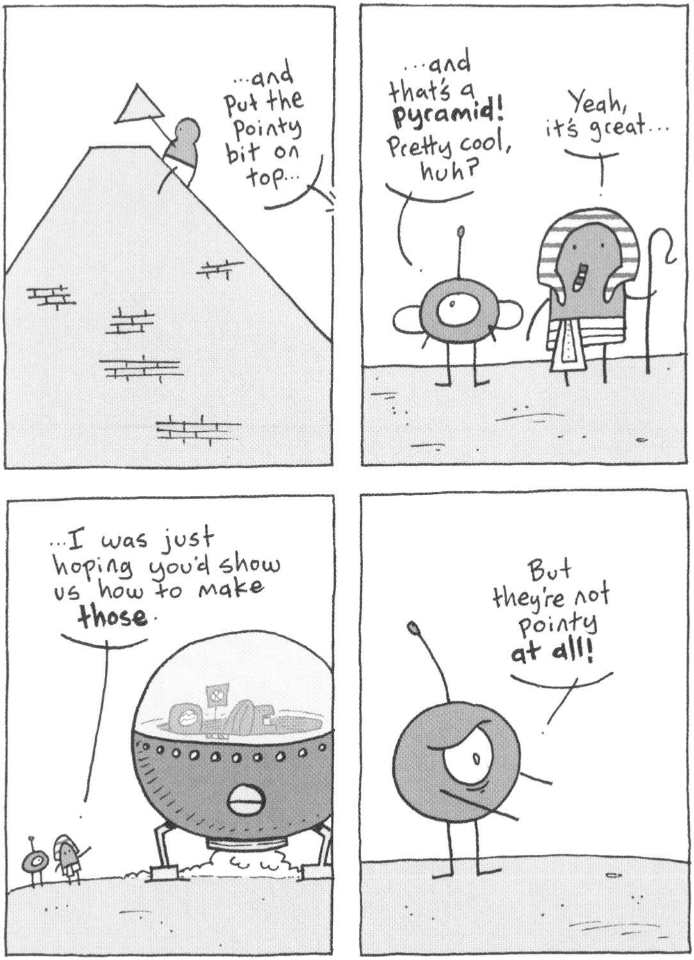
...and put the pointy bit on top...
...and that's a **pyramid!** Pretty cool, huh?
Yeah, it's great...
...I was just hoping you'd show us how to make **those**.
But they're not pointy **at all!**

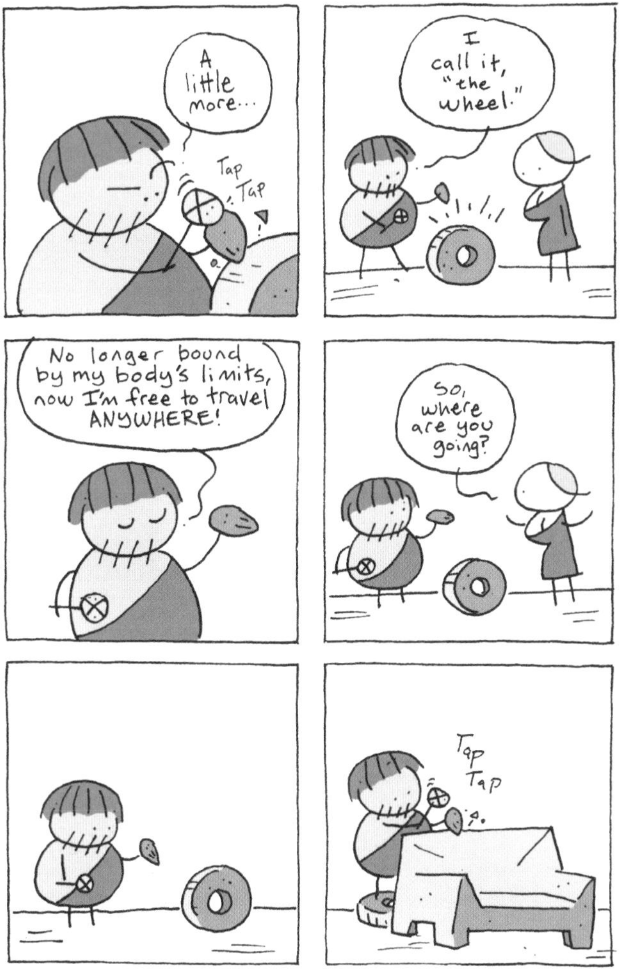
A little more...
Tap Tap
I call it, "the wheel."
No longer bound by my body's limits, now I'm free to travel ANYWHERE!
So, where are you going?
Tap Tap

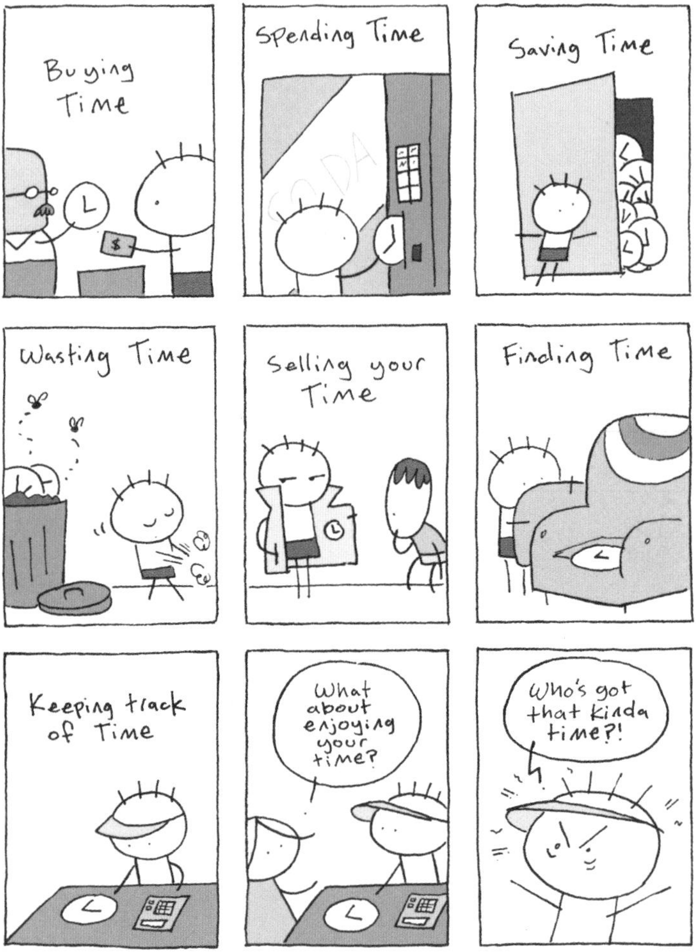
Buying Time
Spending Time
SODA
Saving Time
Wasting Time
Selling your Time
Finding Time
Keeping track of Time
What about enjoying your time?
Who's got that kinda time?!

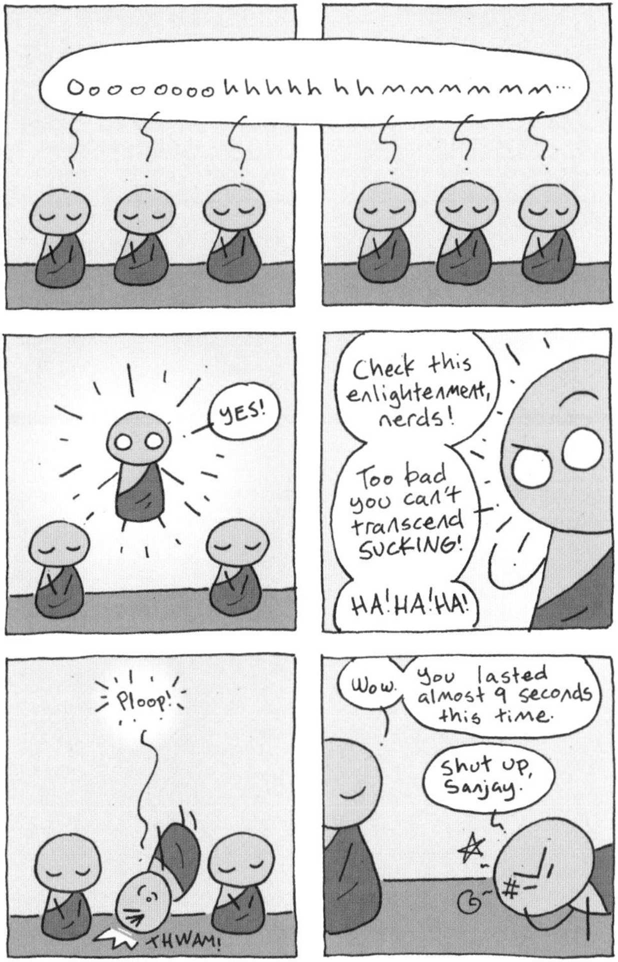
Oooooooohhhhhhhmmmmmmm...
YES!
Check this enlightenment, nerds!
Too bad you can't transcend SUCKING!
HA! HA! HA!
Ploop!
THWAM!
Wow.
You lasted almost 9 seconds this time.
Shut up, Sanjay.

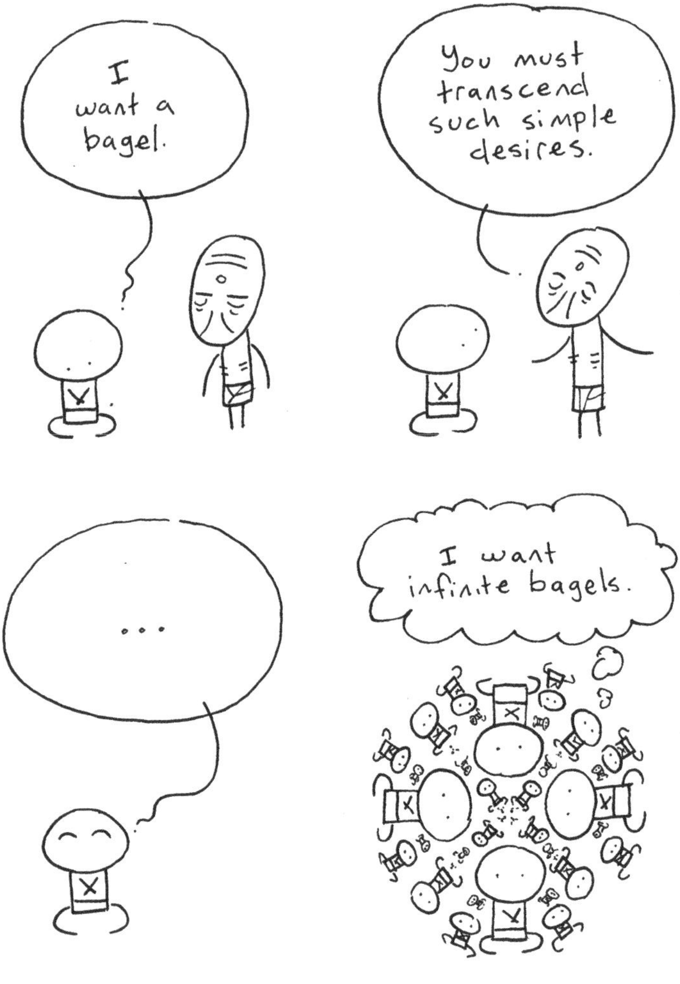
I want a bagel.
You must transcend such simple desires.
...
I want infinite bagels.

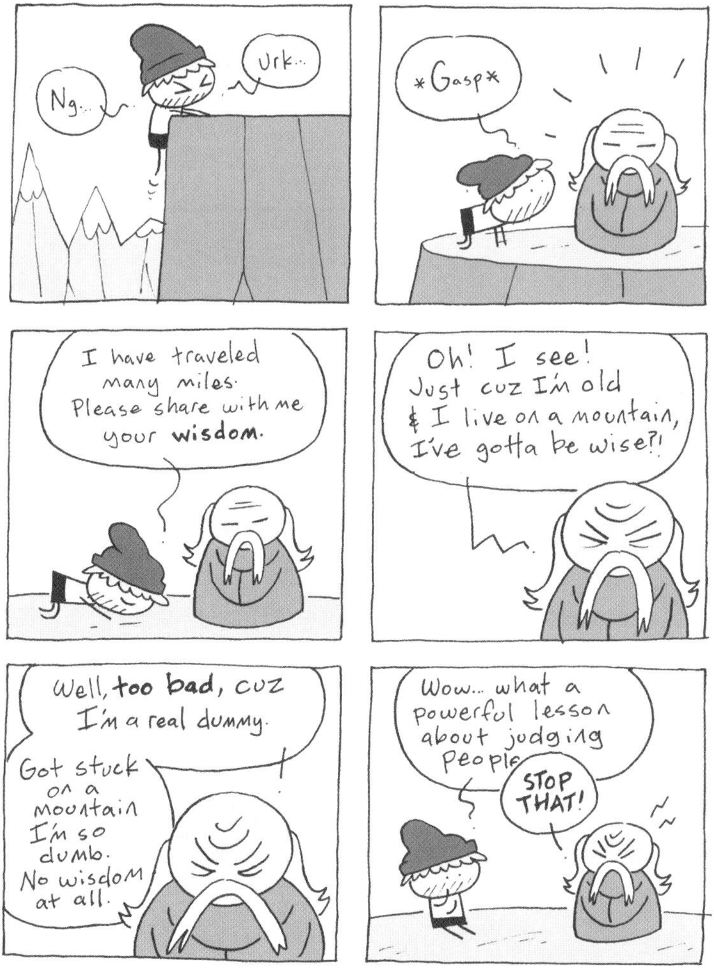
Ng...
Urk...
Gasp
I have traveled many miles. Please share with me your **wisdom**.
Oh! I see! Just cuz I'm old & I live on a mountain, I've gotta be wise?!
Well, **too bad**, cuz I'm a real dummy.
Got stuck on a mountain I'm so dumb. No wisdom at all.
Wow... what a powerful lesson about judging people
STOP THAT!

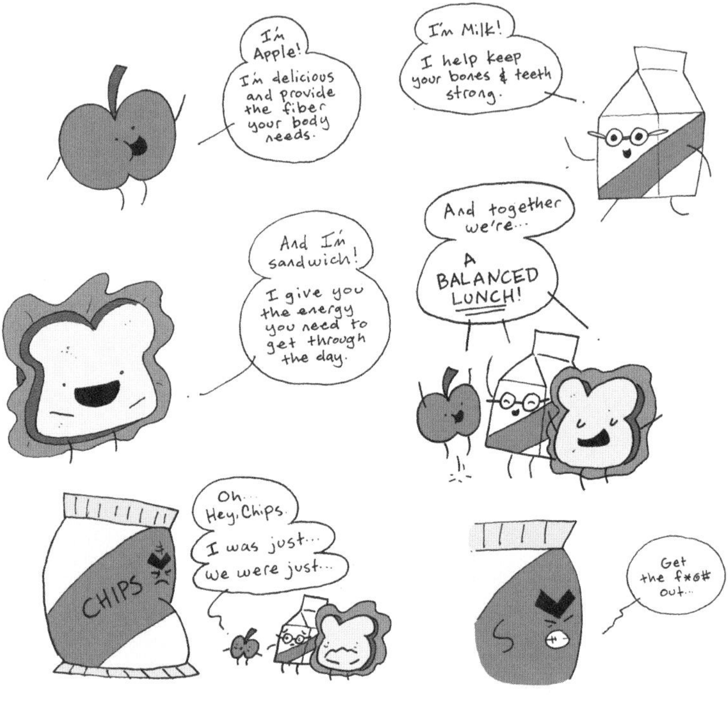
I'm Apple!
I'm delicious and provide the fiber your body needs.
I'm Milk!
I help keep your bones & teeth strong.
And I'm sandwich!
I give you the energy you need to get through the day.
And together we're...
A BALANCED LUNCH!
CHIPS
Oh... Hey, Chips.
I was just...
we were just...
Get the f*@# out...

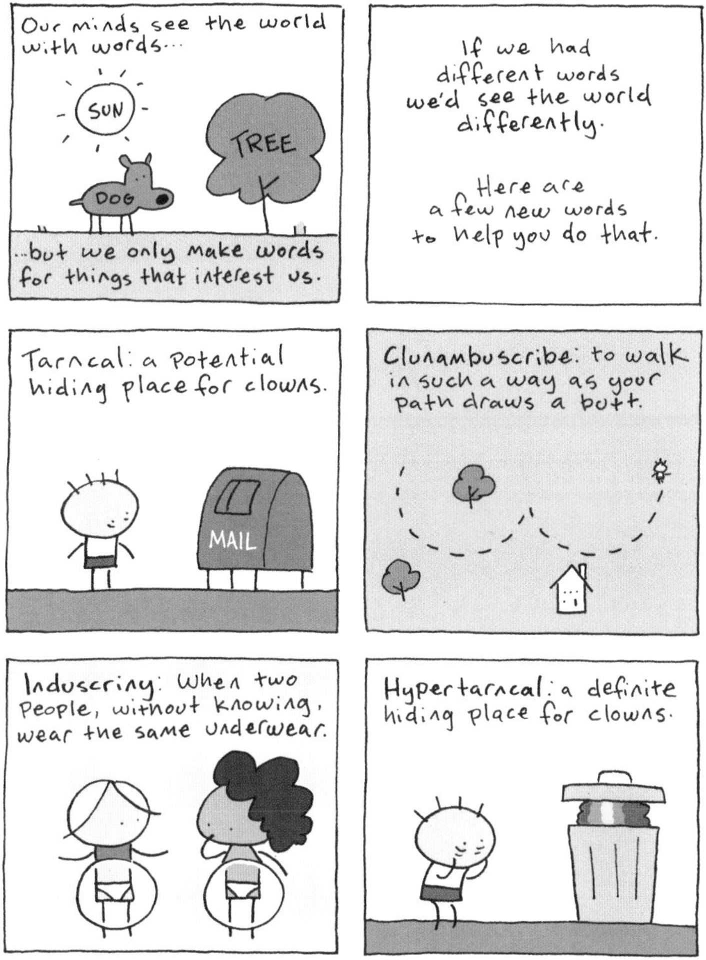
Our minds see the world with words...
SUN
TREE
DOG
...but we only make words for things that interest us.
If we had different words we'd see the world differently.
Here are a few new words to help you do that.
Tarncal: a potential hiding place for clowns.
MAIL
Clunambuscribe: to walk in such a way as your path draws a butt.
Induscring: When two people, without knowing, wear the same underwear.
Hypertarncal: a definite hiding place for clowns.

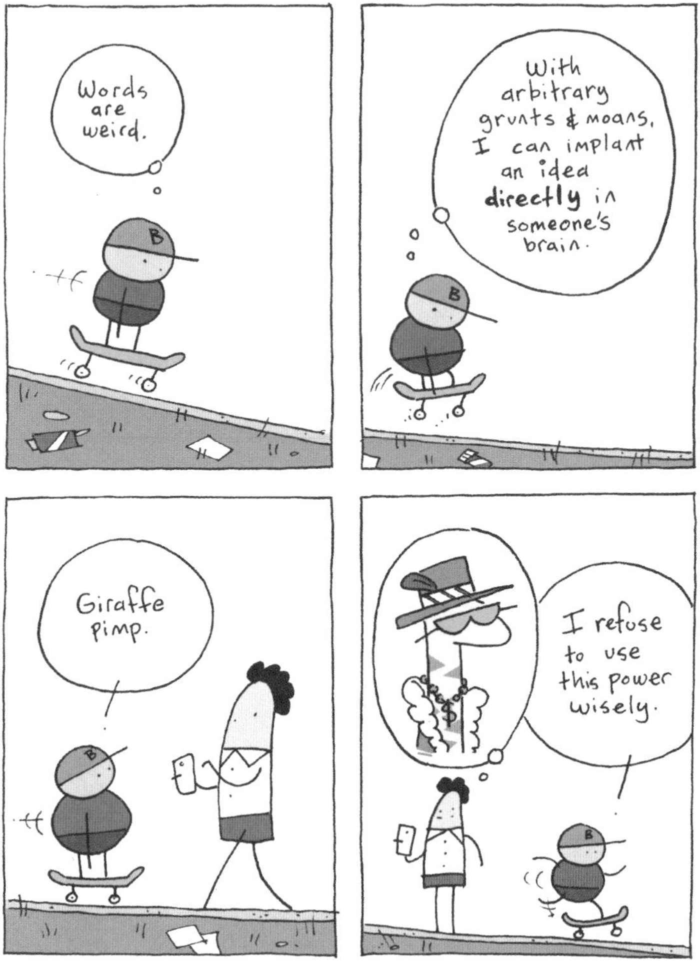
Words are weird.
With arbitrary grunts & moans, I can implant an idea **directly** in someone's brain.
Giraffe pimp.
I refuse to use this power wisely.

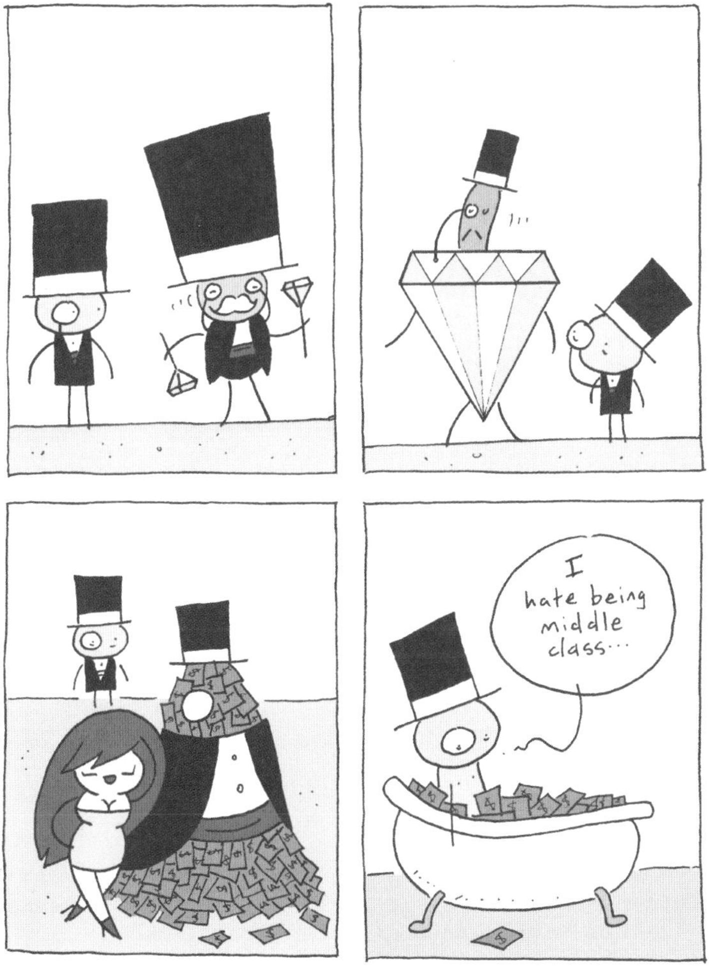
I hate being middle class...

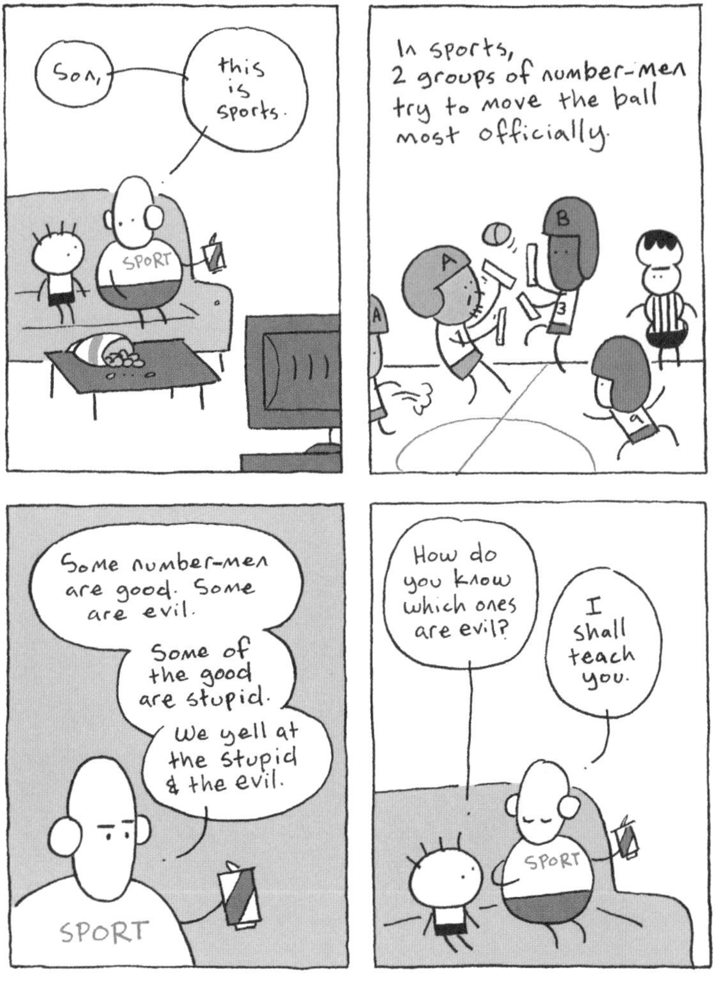
Son,
this is sports.
SPORT
In sports, 2 groups of number-men try to move the ball most officially.
Some number-men are good. Some are evil.
Some of the good are stupid.
We yell at the stupid & the evil.
SPORT
How do you know which ones are evil?
I shall teach you.
SPORT

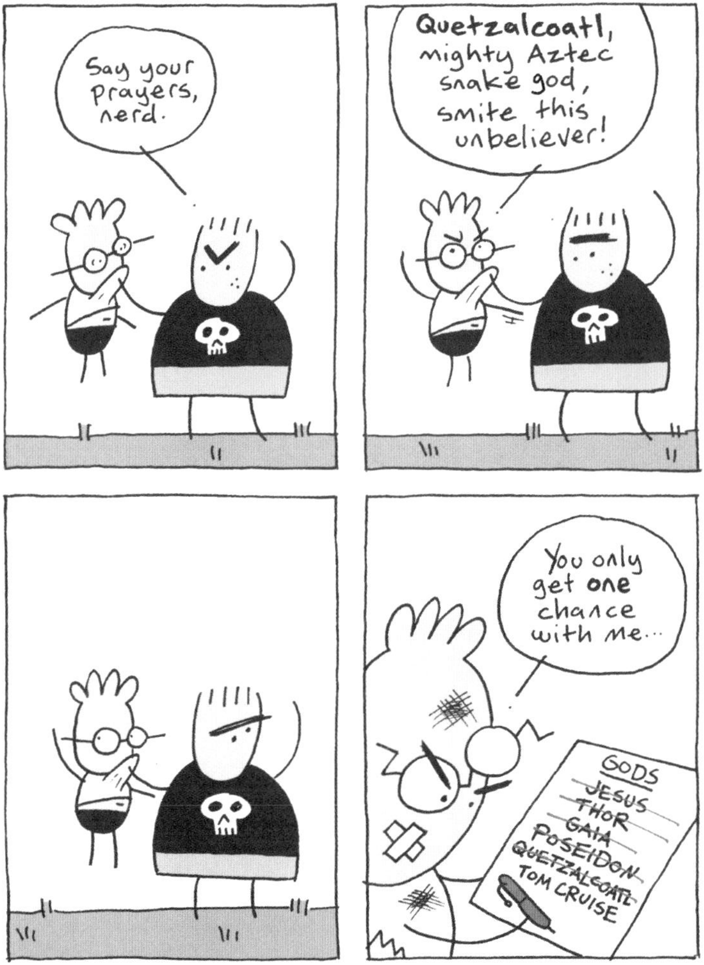

Say your prayers, nerd.
Quetzalcoatl, mighty Aztec snake god, smite this unbeliever!
You only get **one** chance with me...
GODS
JESUS
THOR
GAIA
POSEIDON
QUETZALCOATL
TOM CRUISE

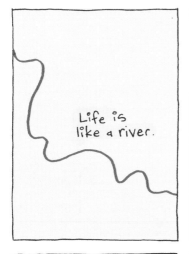

Life is like a river.

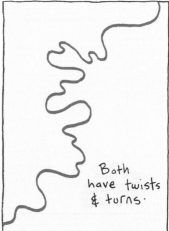

Both have twists & turns.

Both can take many paths...

...but all lead to the same inevitable end.

Plus, both go through that stoner phase.

REINCARNATION

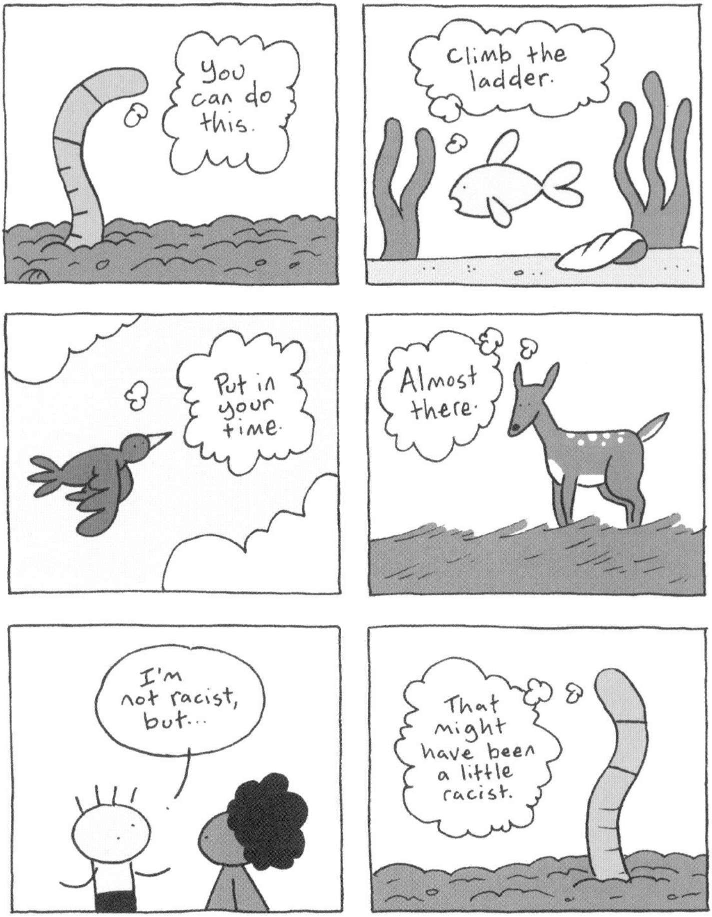
You can do this.
Climb the ladder.
Put in your time.
Almost there.
I'm not racist, but...
That might have been a little racist.

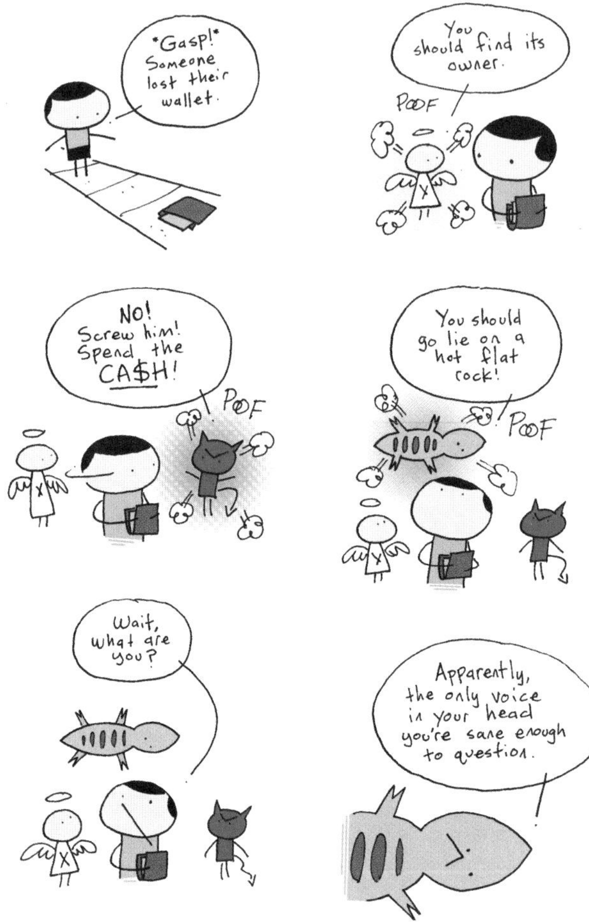
Gasp! Someone lost their wallet.
You should find its owner.
POOF
NO! Screw him! Spend the CA$H!
POOF
You should go lie on a hot flat rock!
POOF
Wait, what are you?
Apparently, the only voice in your head you're sane enough to question.

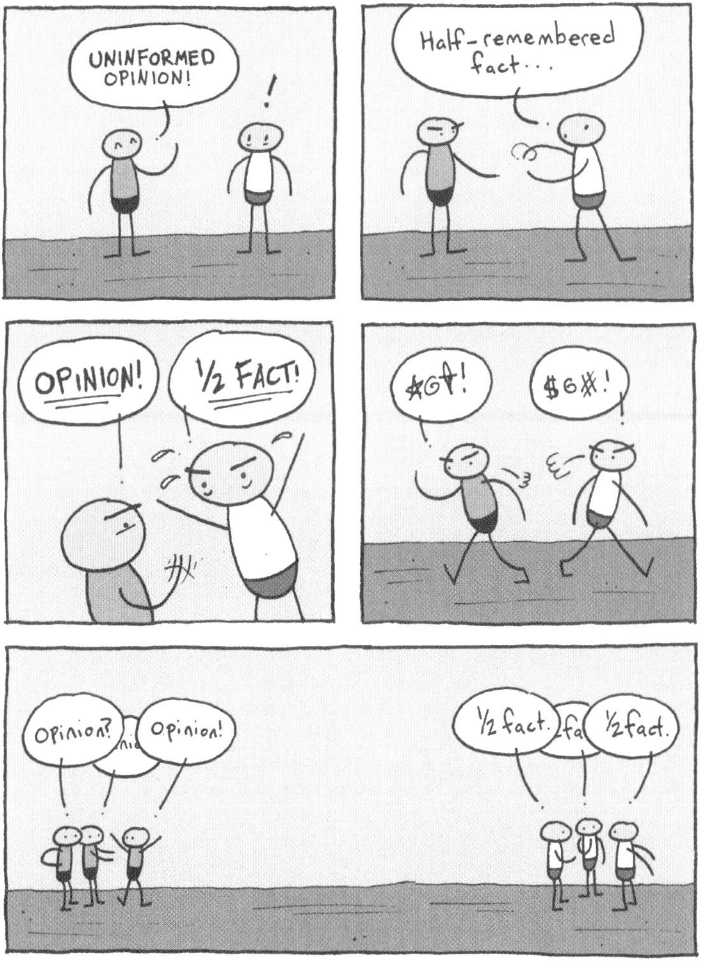
UNINFORMED OPINION!
!
Half-remembered fact...
OPINION!
1/2 FACT!
Opinion?
Opinion!
1/2 fact.
1/2 fact.

OPTIMISTS VS EXTREMISTS

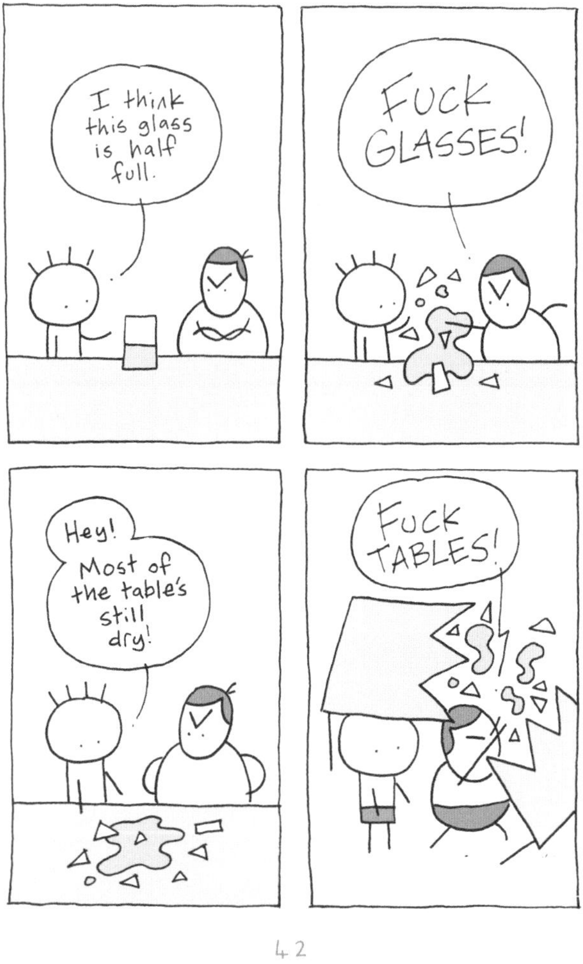
I think this glass is half full.
FUCK GLASSES!
Hey!
Most of the table's still dry!
FUCK TABLES!

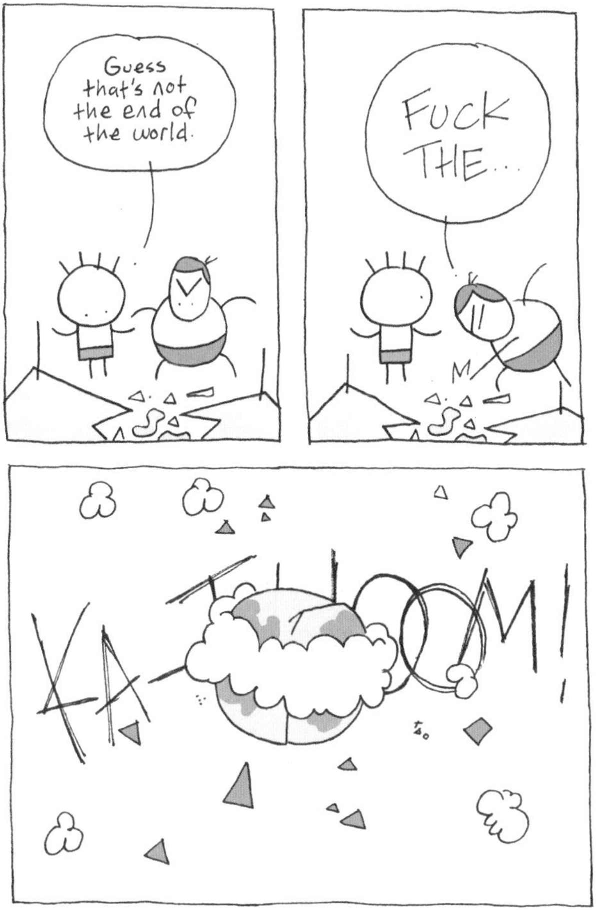
Guess that's not the end of the world.
FUCK THE...
KA-THOOM!

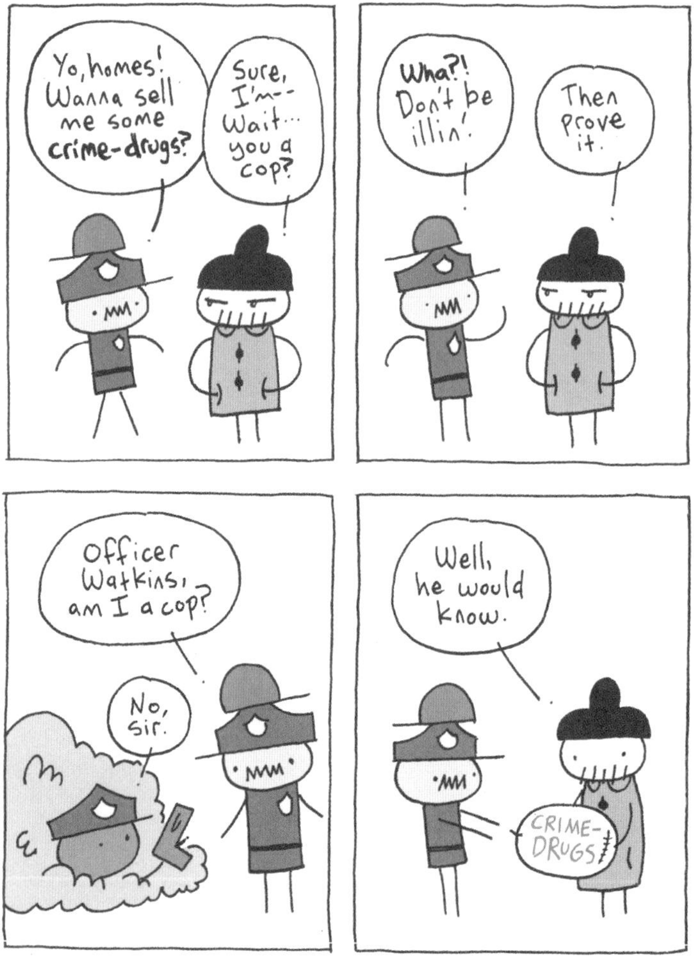
Yo, homes! Wanna sell me some crime-drugs?
Sure, I'm-- Wait... you a cop?
Wha?! Don't be illin'!
Then prove it.
Officer Watkins, am I a cop?
No, sir.
Well, he would know.
CRIME-DRUGS

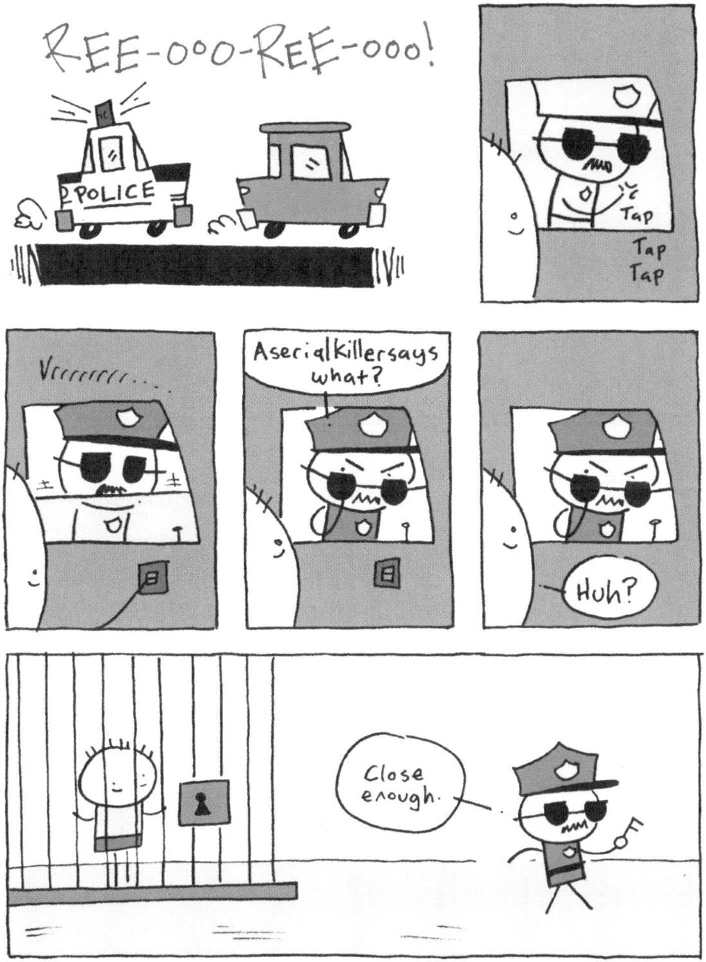
REE-ooo-REE-ooo!
POLICE
Tap
Tap
Tap
Vrrrrrrr....
Aserialkillersays what?
Huh?
Close enough.

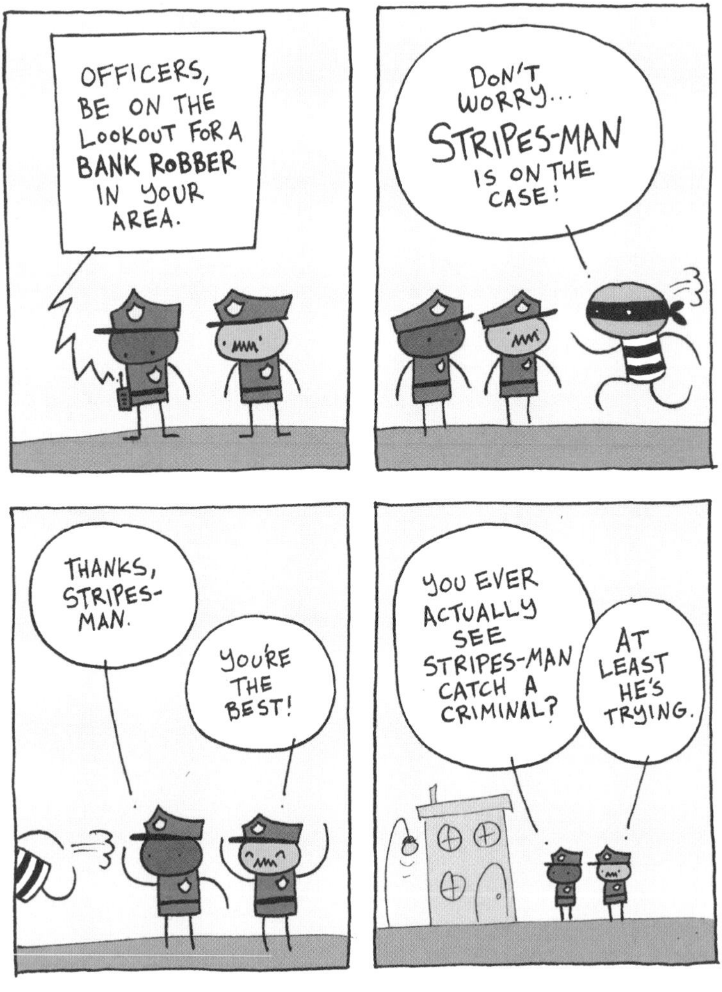
OFFICERS, BE ON THE LOOKOUT FOR A BANK ROBBER IN YOUR AREA.
DON'T WORRY... STRIPES-MAN IS ON THE CASE!
THANKS, STRIPES-MAN.
YOU'RE THE BEST!
YOU EVER ACTUALLY SEE STRIPES-MAN CATCH A CRIMINAL?
AT LEAST HE'S TRYING.

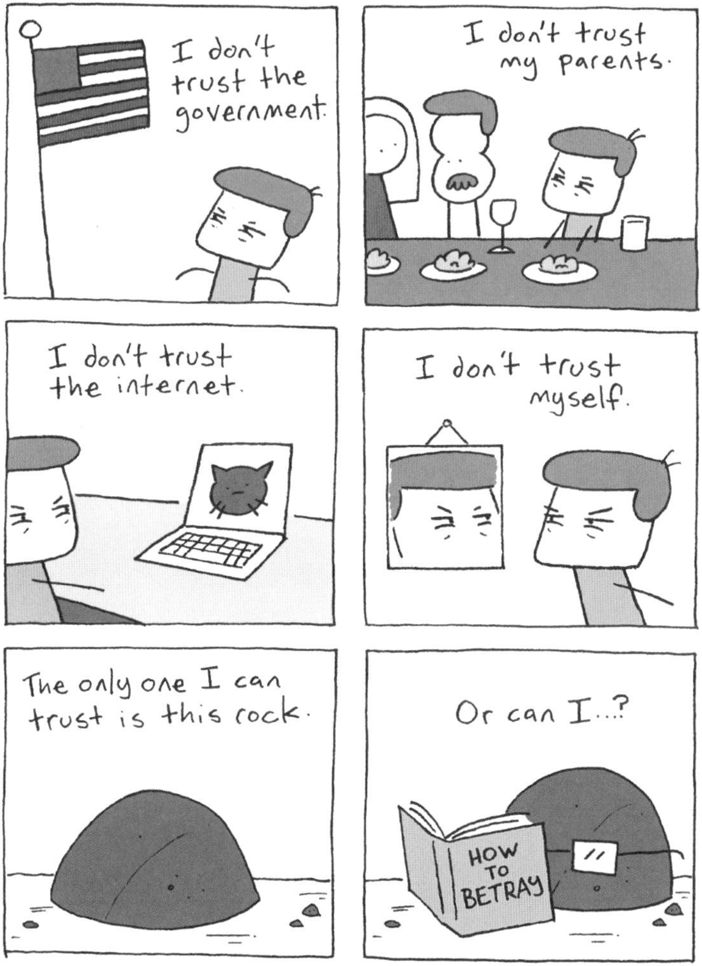
I don't trust the government.
I don't trust my parents.
I don't trust the internet.
I don't trust myself.
The only one I can trust is this rock.
Or can I...?
HOW TO BETRAY

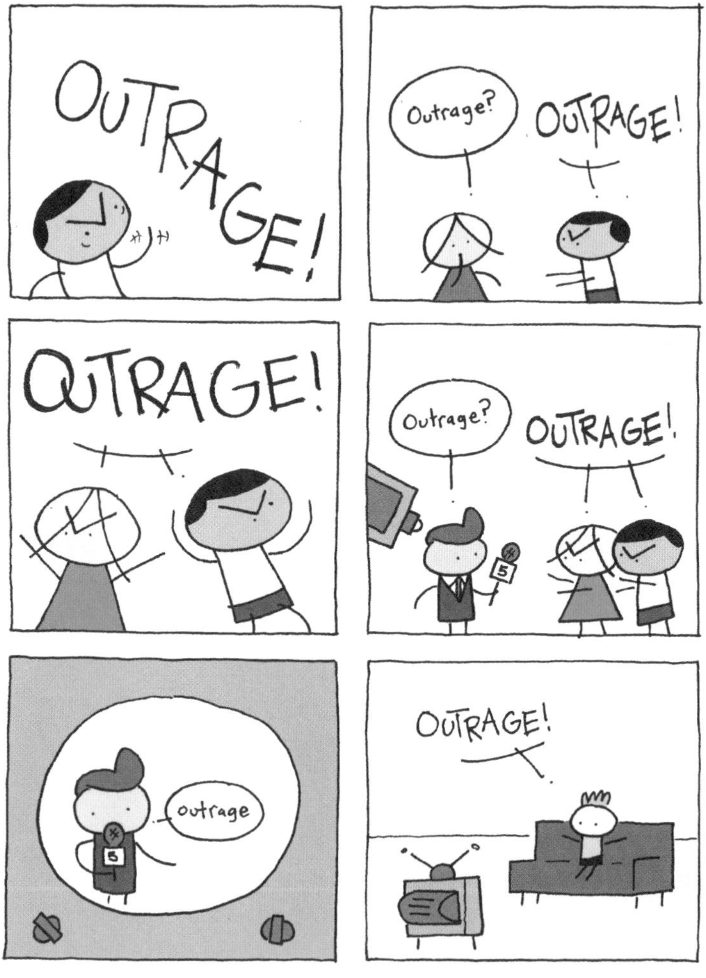
OUTRAGE!
Outrage?
OUTRAGE!
OUTRAGE!
Outrage?
OUTRAGE!
outrage
OUTRAGE!

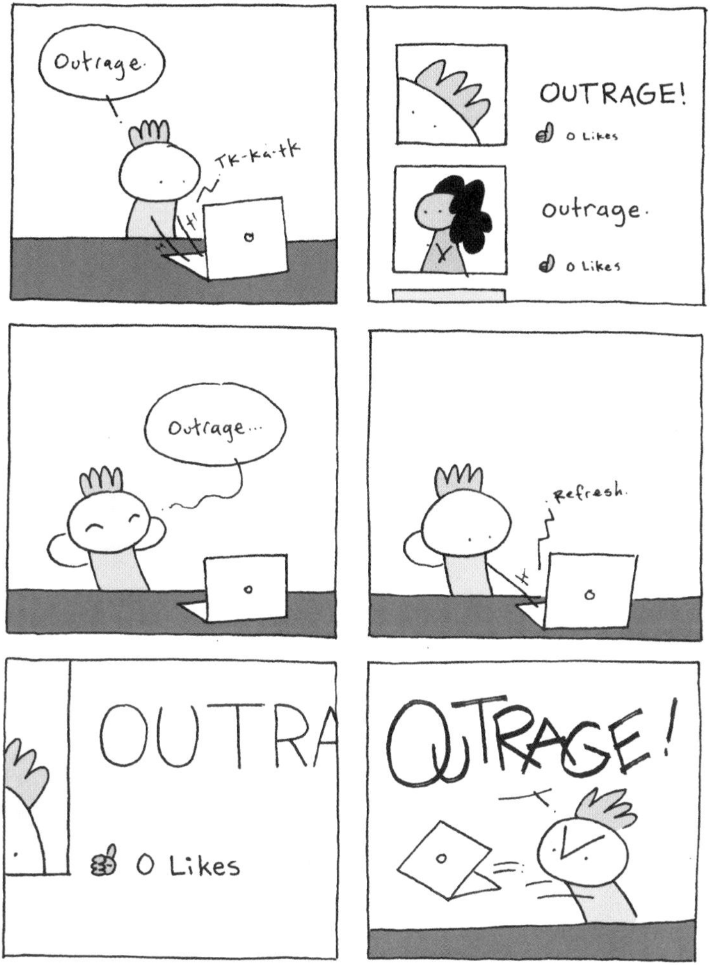
Outrage.
TK-ka-tk
OUTRAGE!
0 Likes
outrage.
0 Likes
Outrage...
Refresh.
OUTRA
0 Likes
OUTRAGE!

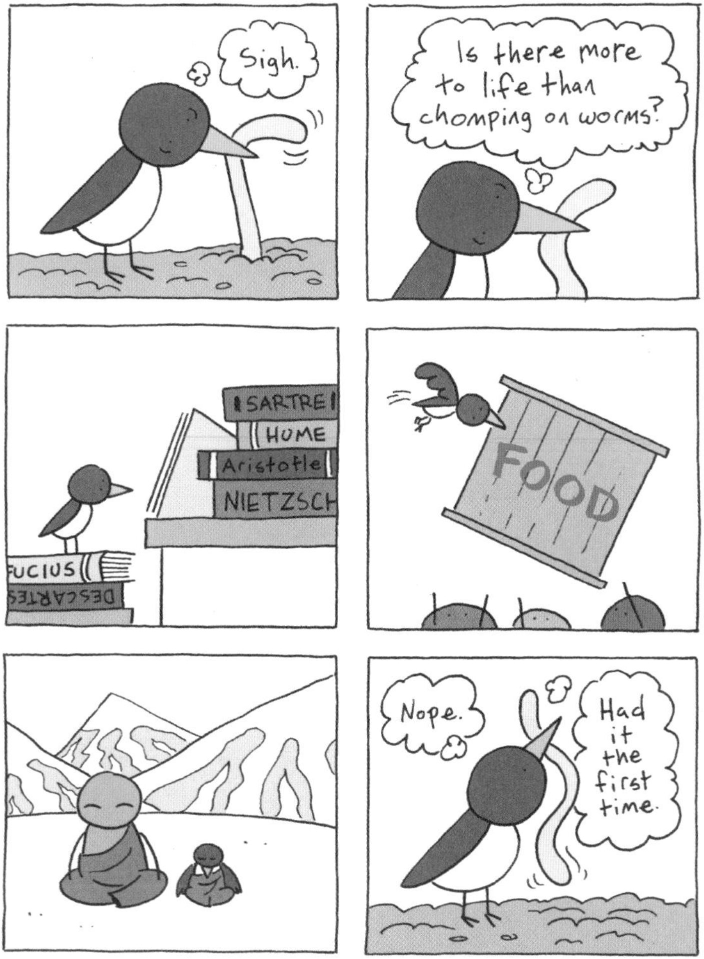
Sigh.
Is there more to life than chomping on worms?
SARTRE
HUME
Aristotle
NIETZSCH
FUCIUS
DESCARTES
FOOD
Nope.
Had it the first time.

Zoology

ROYALTY IN THE ANIMAL WORLD

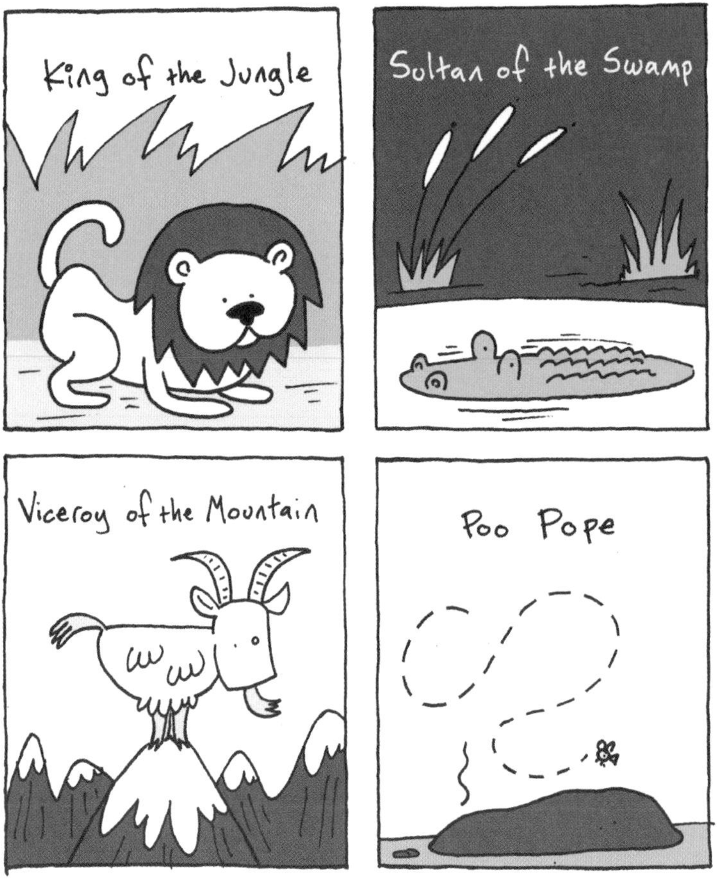
King of the Jungle
Sultan of the Swamp
Viceroy of the Mountain
Poo Pope

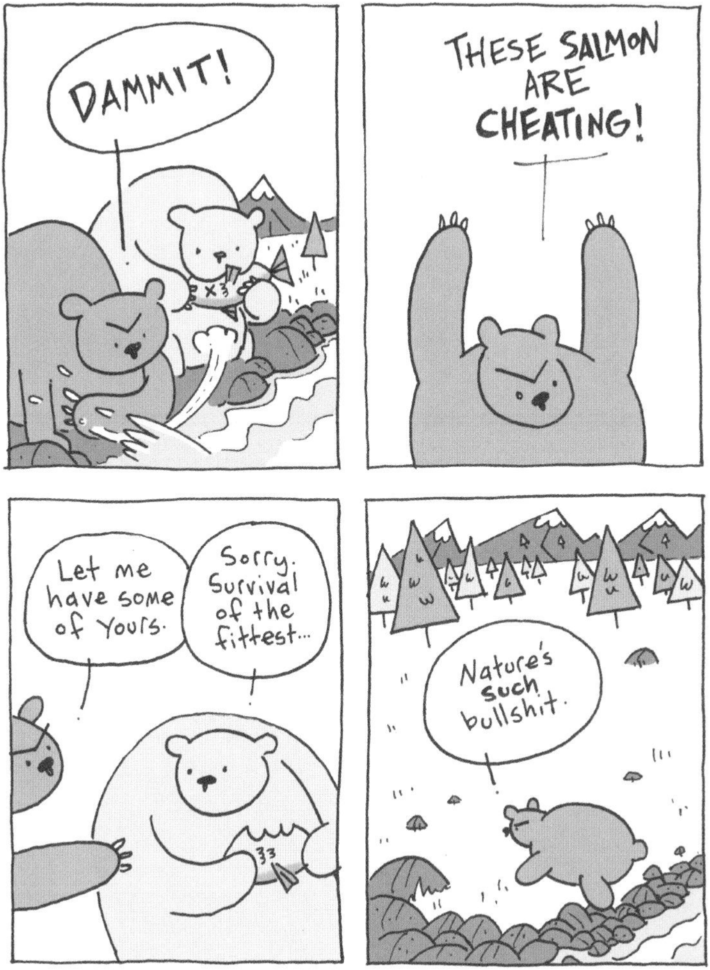
DAMMIT!
THESE SALMON ARE CHEATING!
Let me have some of yours.
Sorry. Survival of the fittest...
Nature's such bullshit.

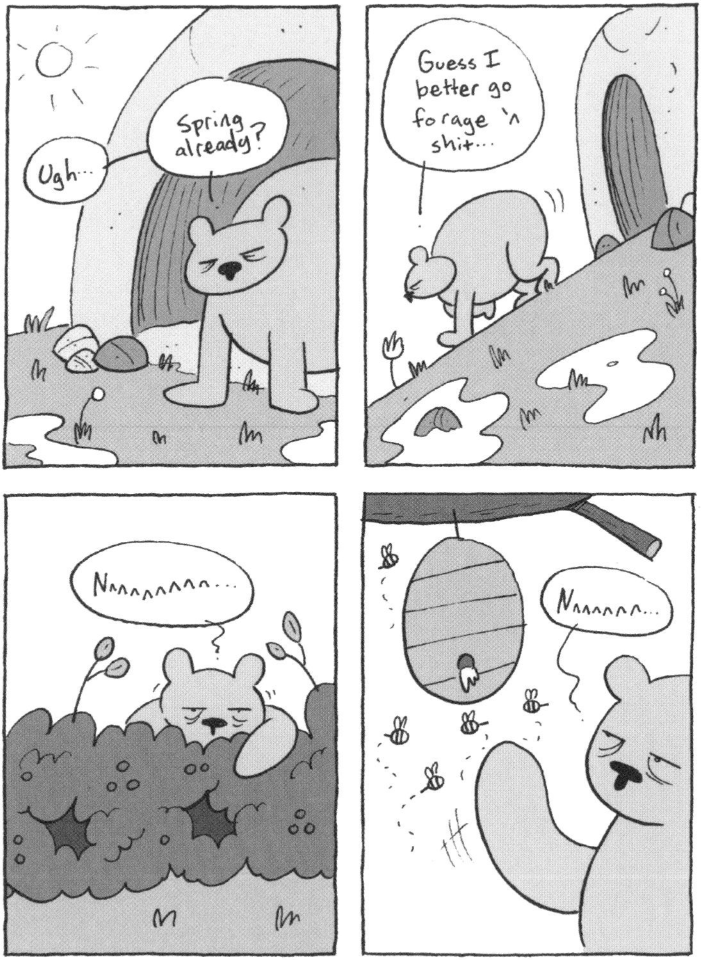
Ugh...
Spring already?
Guess I better go forage 'n shit...
Nʌʌʌʌʌʌʌʌ...
Nʌʌʌʌʌʌ...

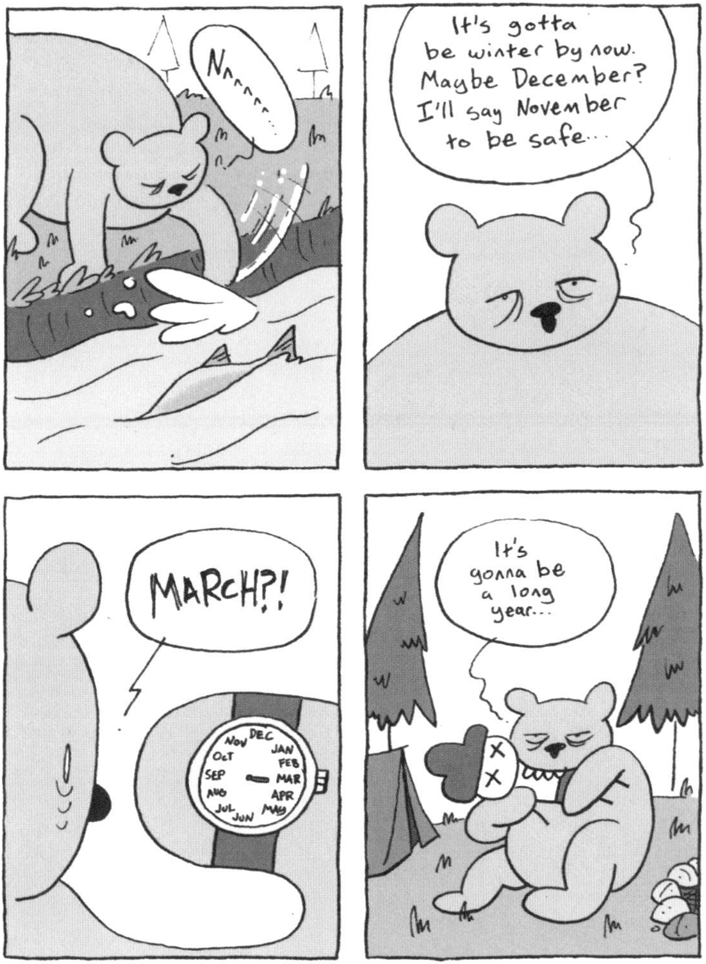
Nnnnnnn.....
It's gotta be winter by now. Maybe December? I'll say November to be safe...
MARCH?!
NOV DEC JAN OCT FEB SEP MAR AUG APR JUL JUN MAY
It's gonna be a long year...

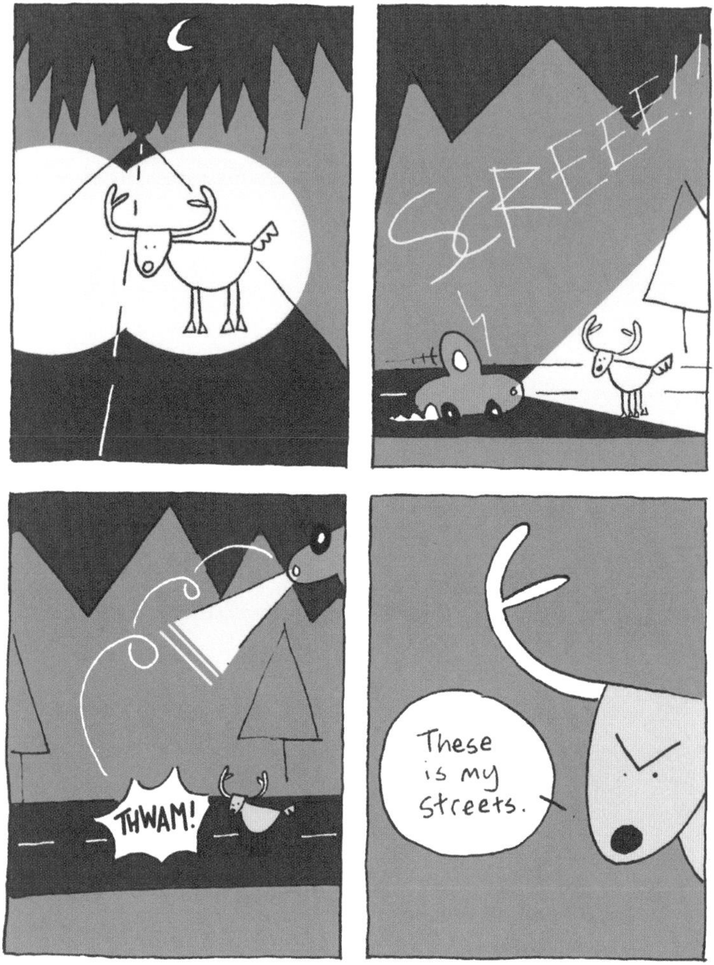
SCREEE!!
THWAM!
These is my streets.

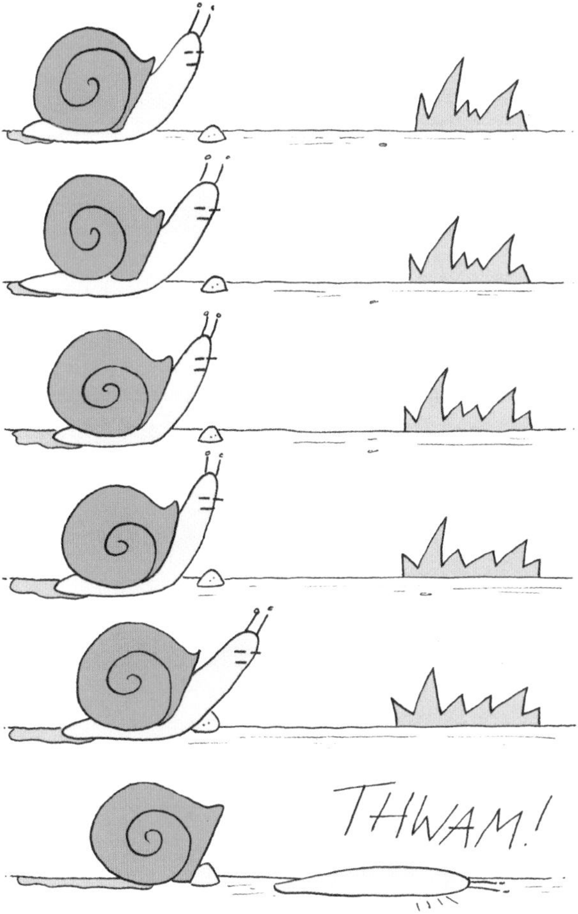
THWAM!

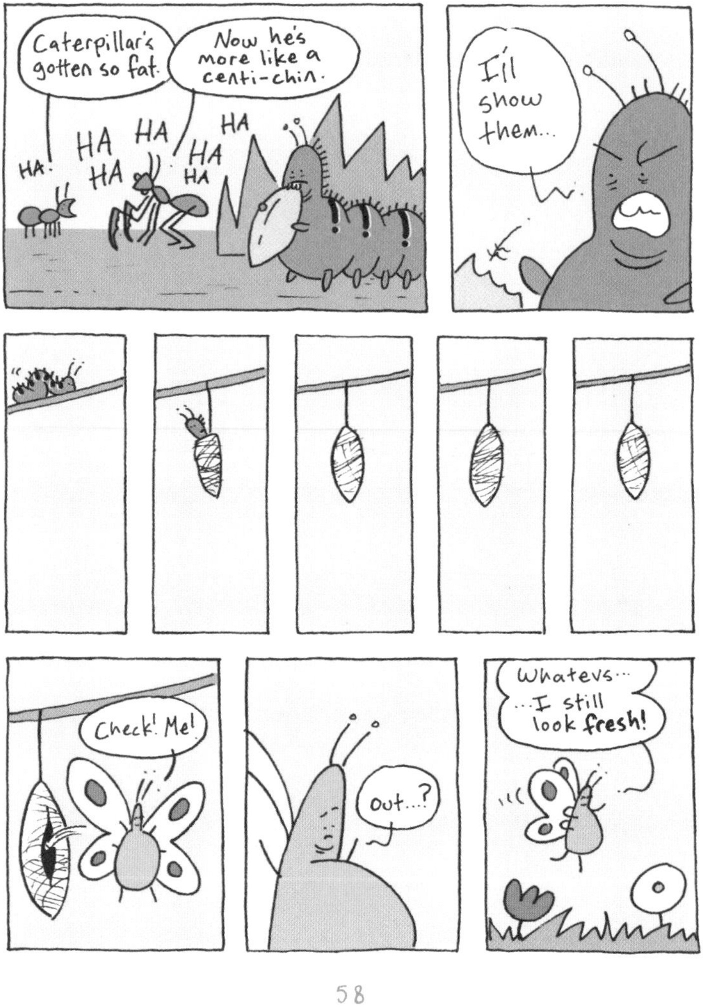
Caterpillar's gotten so fat.
Now he's more like a centi-chin.
HA!
HA HA
HA
HA HA
HA
HA
I'll show them...
Check! Me!
out...?
Whatevs...
...I still look **fresh!**

Nature is about balance.

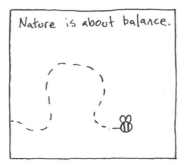

The flower provides pollen to the bee.

The bee gives the flower seven dollars.

The flower saves up enough for an iPhone.

The bee's Apple stock goes up.

The flower listens to Coldplay.

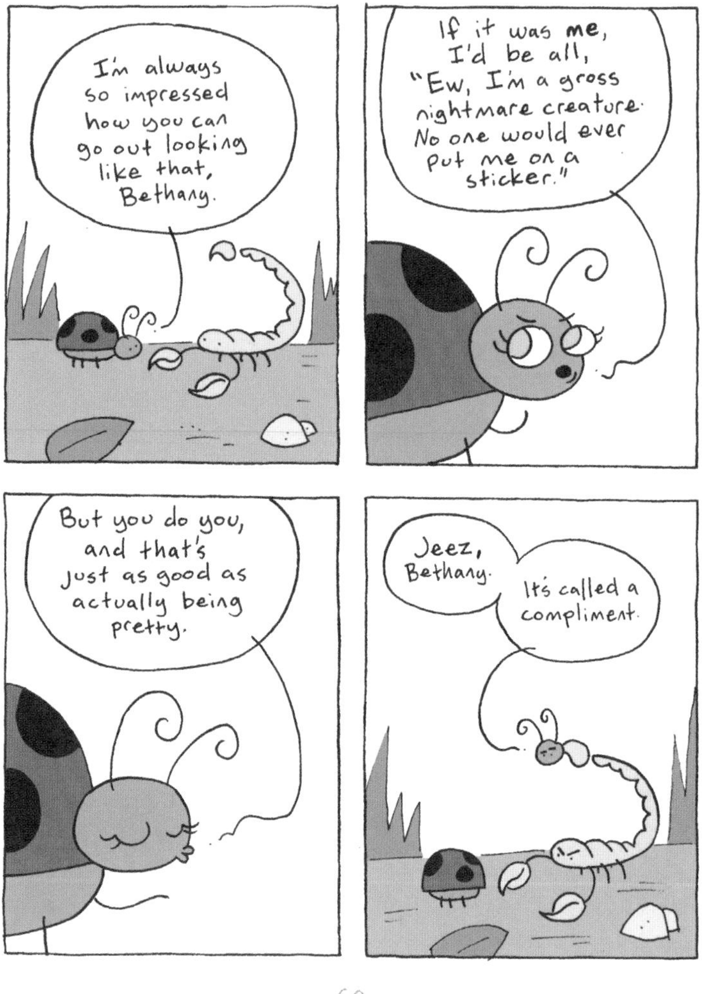
I'm always so impressed how you can go out looking like that, Bethany.
If it was **me**, I'd be all, "Ew, I'm a gross nightmare creature. No one would ever put me on a sticker."
But you do you, and that's just as good as actually being pretty.
Jeez, Bethany.
It's called a compliment.

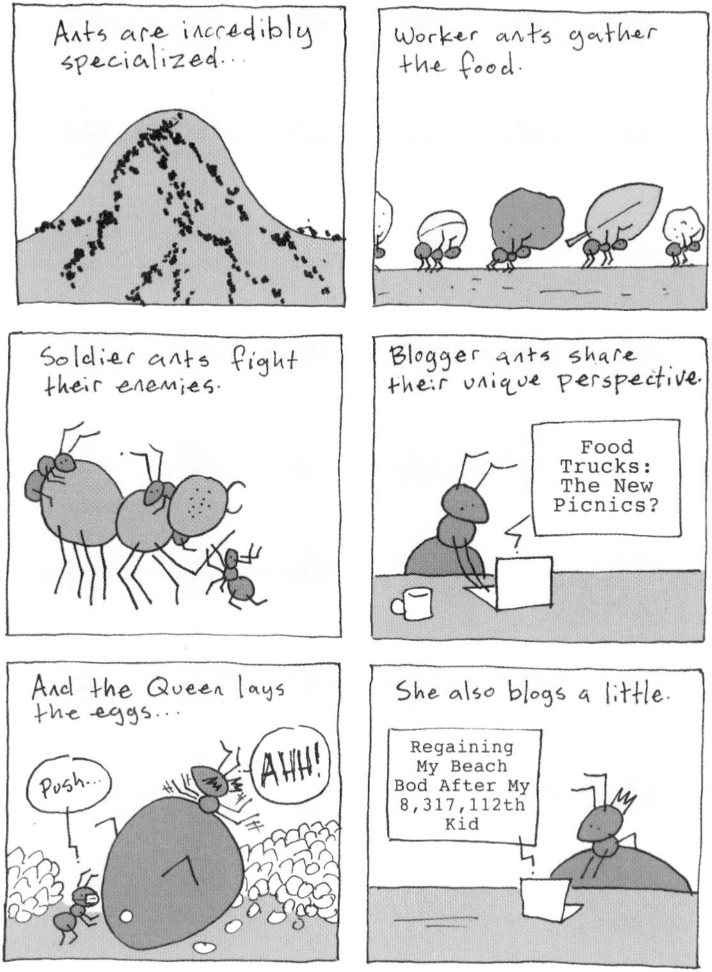
Ants are incredibly specialized...
Worker ants gather the food.
Soldier ants fight their enemies.
Blogger ants share their unique perspective.
Food Trucks: The New Picnics?
And the Queen lays the eggs...
Push...
AHH!
She also blogs a little.
Regaining My Beach Bod After My 8,317,112th Kid

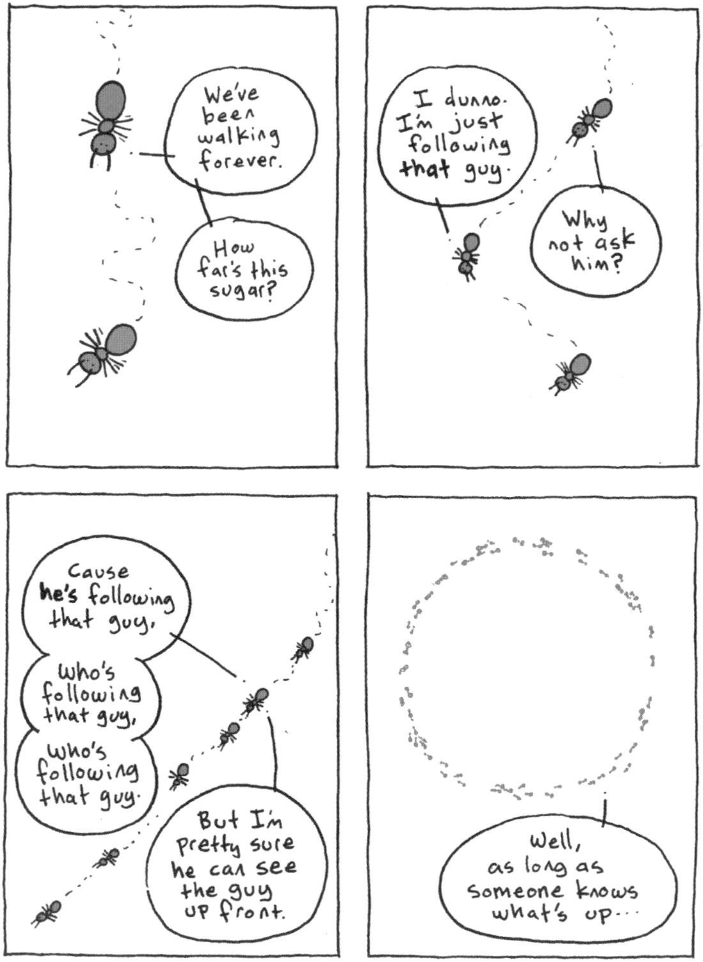
We've been walking forever.
How far's this sugar?
I dunno. I'm just following that guy.
Why not ask him?
Cause he's following that guy,
who's following that guy,
who's following that guy.
But I'm pretty sure he can see the guy up front.
Well, as long as someone knows what's up...

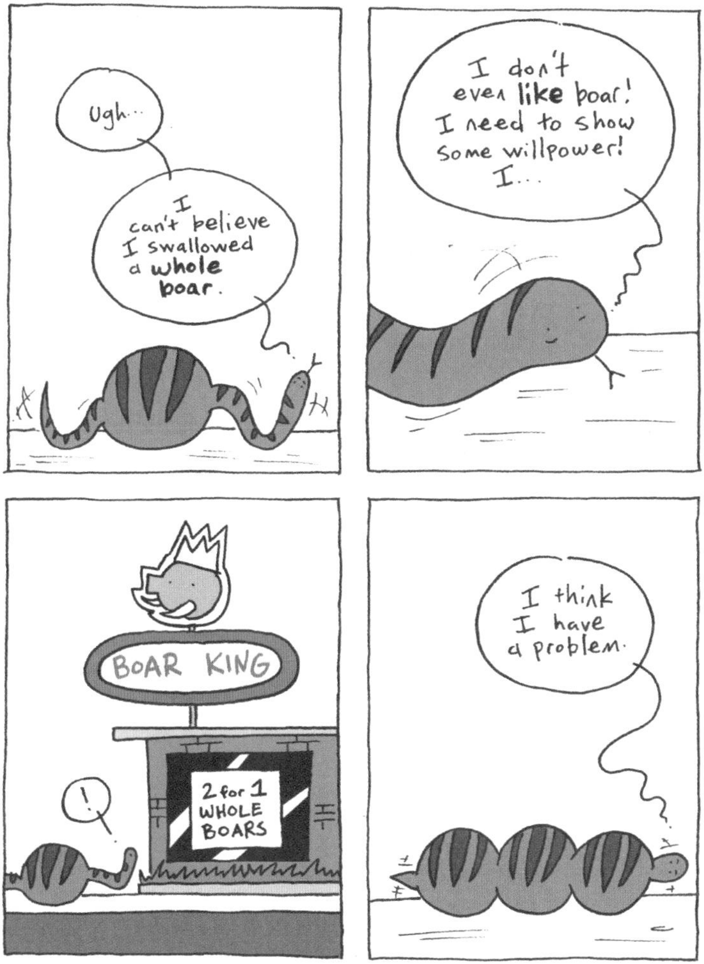
Ugh...
I can't believe I swallowed a **whole** boar.
I don't even **like** boar! I need to show some willpower! I...
BOAR KING
!
2 for 1 WHOLE BOARS
I think I have a problem.

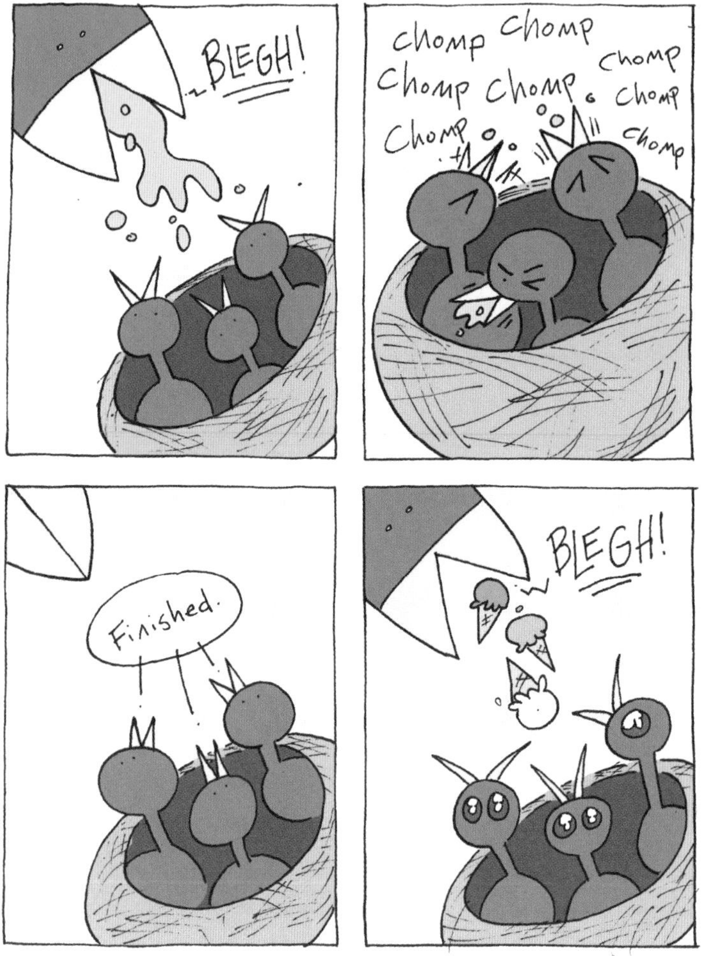
BLEGH!
Chomp Chomp
Chomp Chomp
Chomp
Chomp
Chomp
Chomp
Finished.
BLEGH!

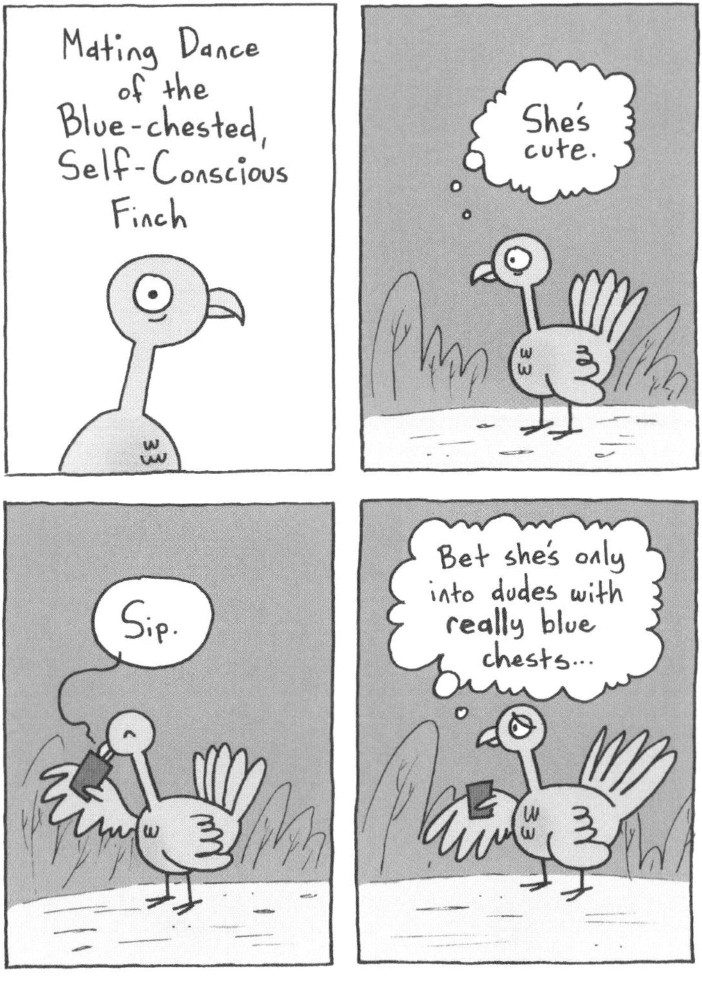
Mating Dance of the Blue-chested, Self-Conscious Finch
She's cute.
Sip.
Bet she's only into dudes with **really** blue chests...

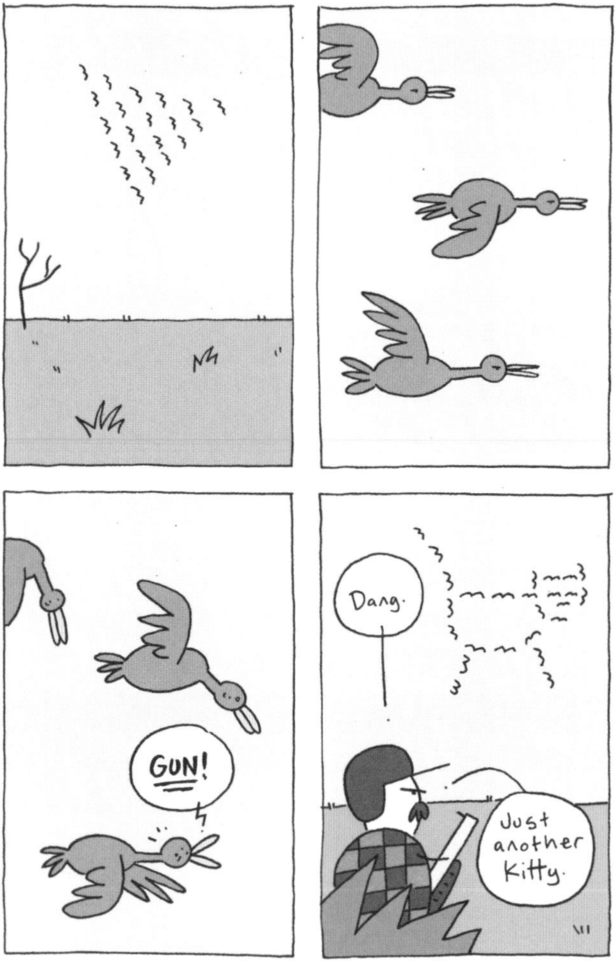

GUN!
Dang.
Just another Kitty.

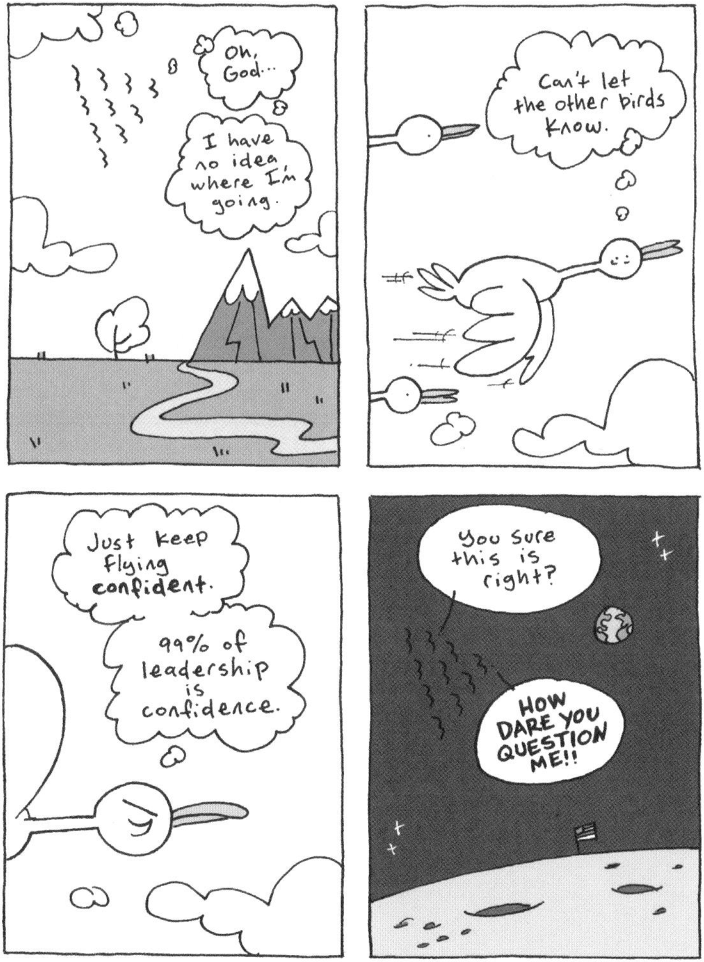
Oh, God...
I have no idea where I'm going.
Can't let the other birds know.
Just keep flying **confident**.
99% of leadership is confidence.
You sure this is right?
HOW DARE YOU QUESTION ME!!

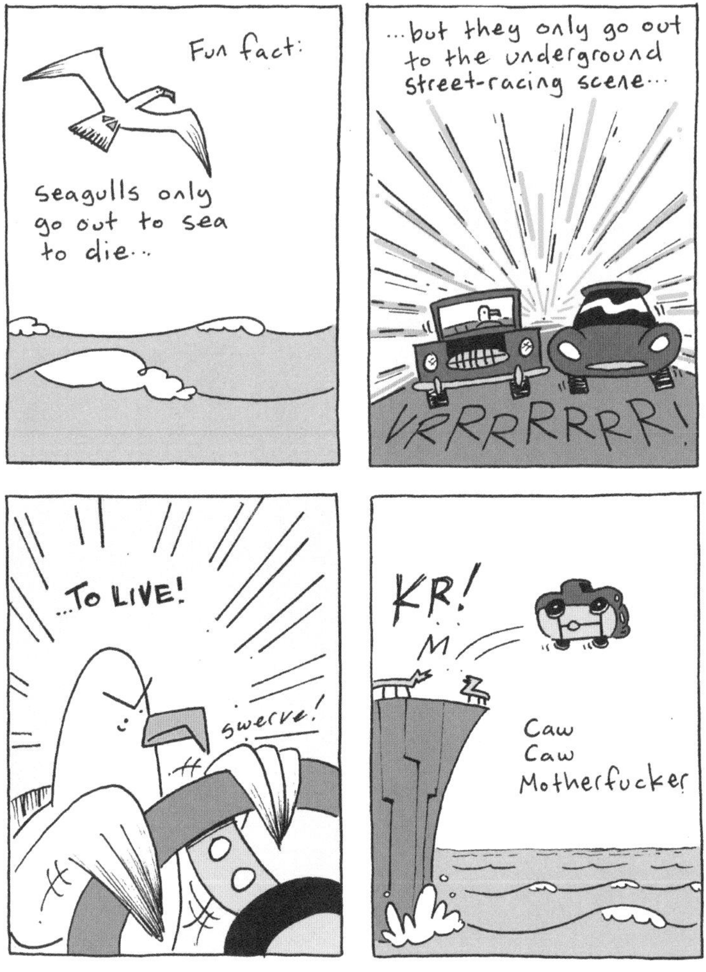

Fun fact:
Seagulls only go out to sea to die...
...but they only go out to the underground street-racing scene...
VRRRRRRR!
...TO LIVE!
swerve!
KR!
M
Caw
Caw
Motherfucker

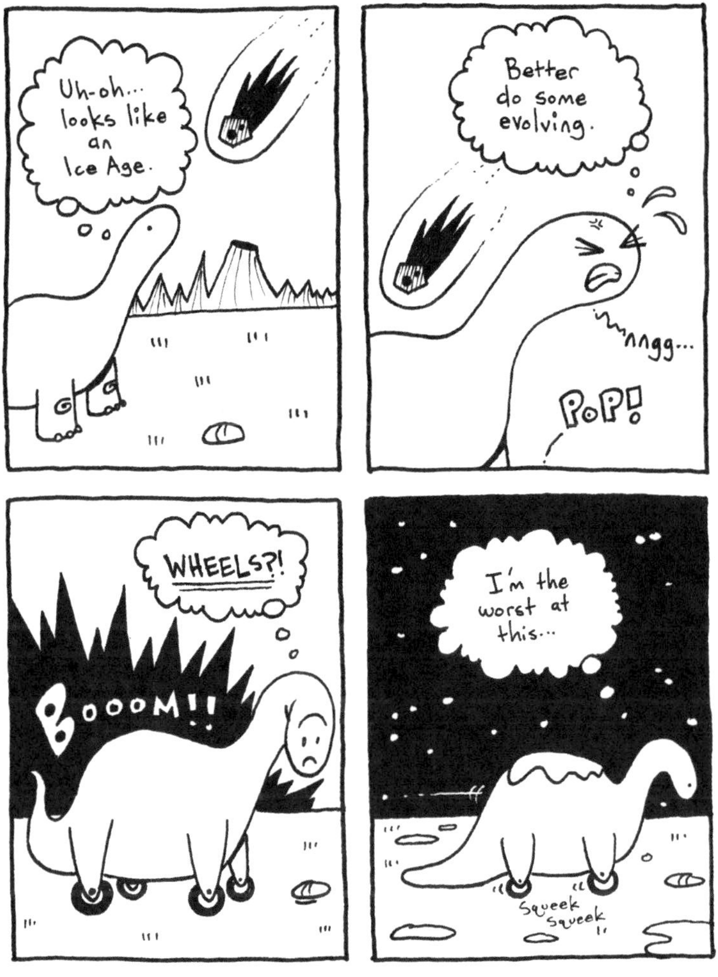
Uh-oh...
looks like
an
Ice Age.
Better
do some
evolving.
nngg...
POP!
WHEELS?!
BOOOM!!
I'm the
worst at
this...
Squeek
Squeek

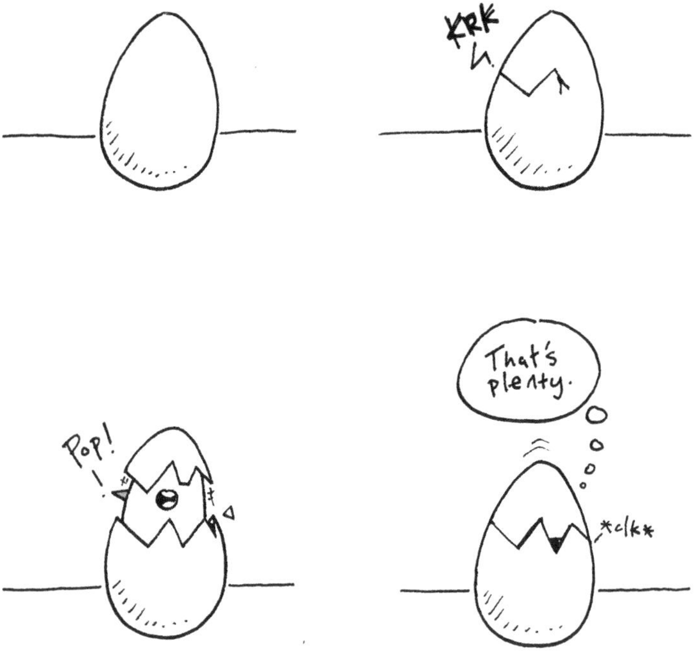
KRK
Pop!
That's plenty.
clk

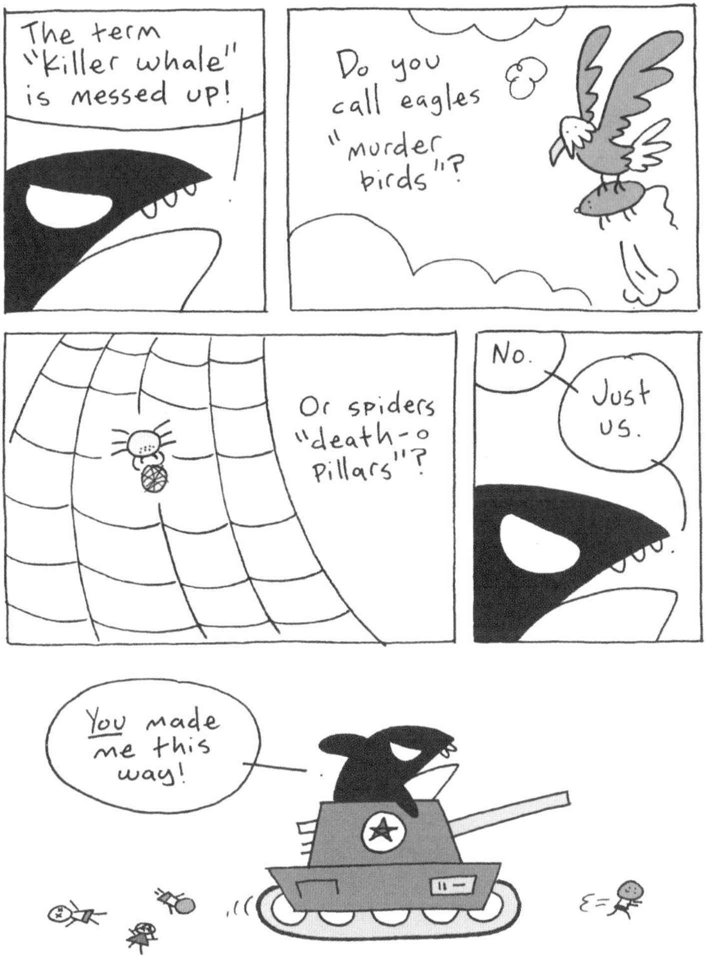
The term "Killer whale" is messed up!
Do you call eagles "murder birds"?
Or spiders "death-o pillars"?
No.
Just us.
You made me this way!

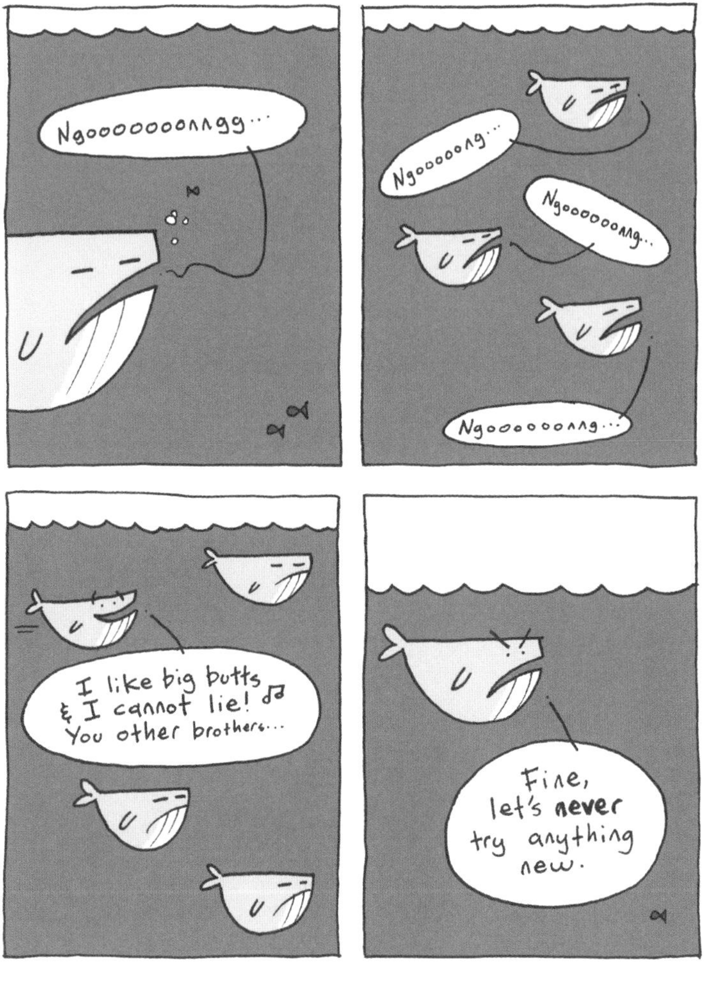
Ngoooooooonngg...
Ngooooong...
Ngoooooong...
Ngoooooonng...
I like big butts & I cannot lie! You other brothers...
Fine, let's **never** try anything new.

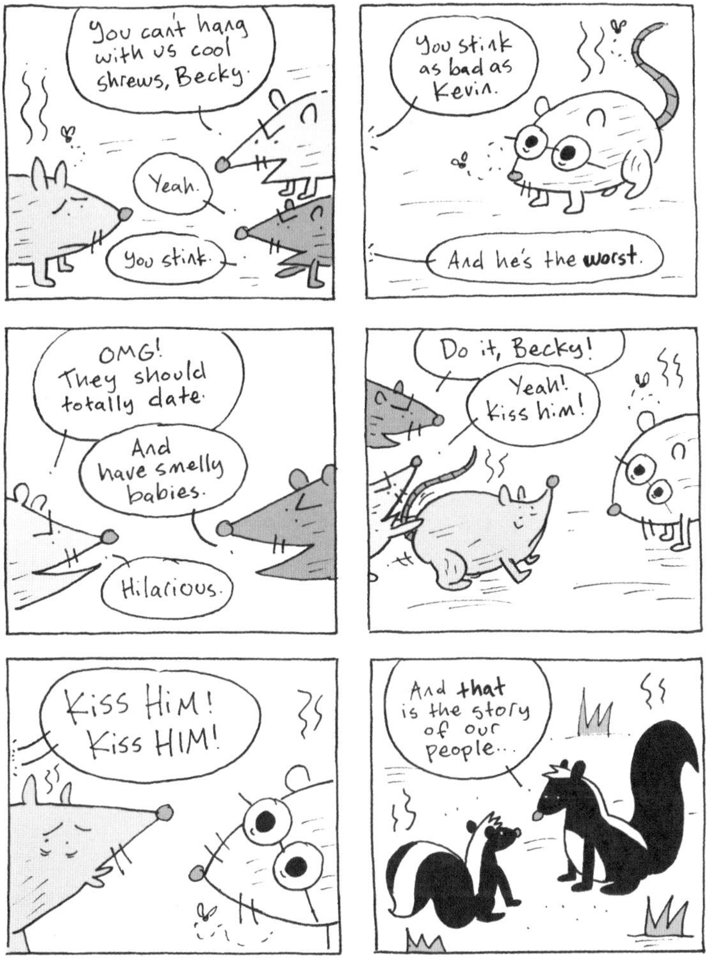
You can't hang with us cool shrews, Becky.
Yeah.
You stink.
You stink as bad as Kevin.
And he's the **worst**.
OMG! They should totally date.
And have smelly babies.
Hilarious.
Do it, Becky!
Yeah! Kiss him!
Kiss HIM! Kiss HIM!
And **that** is the story of our people...

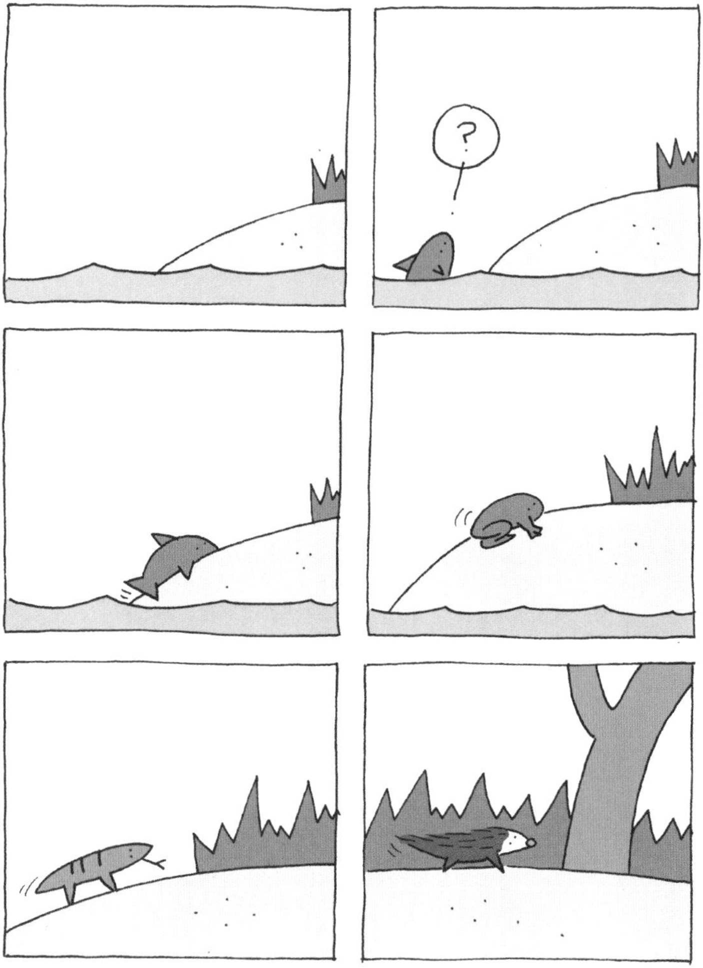
?

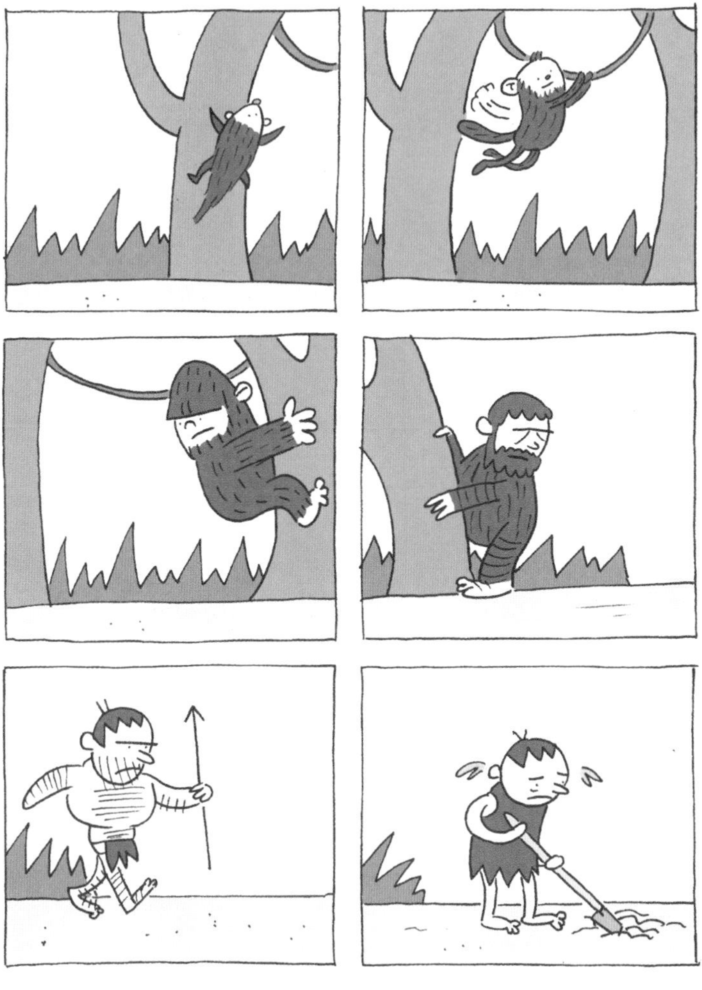

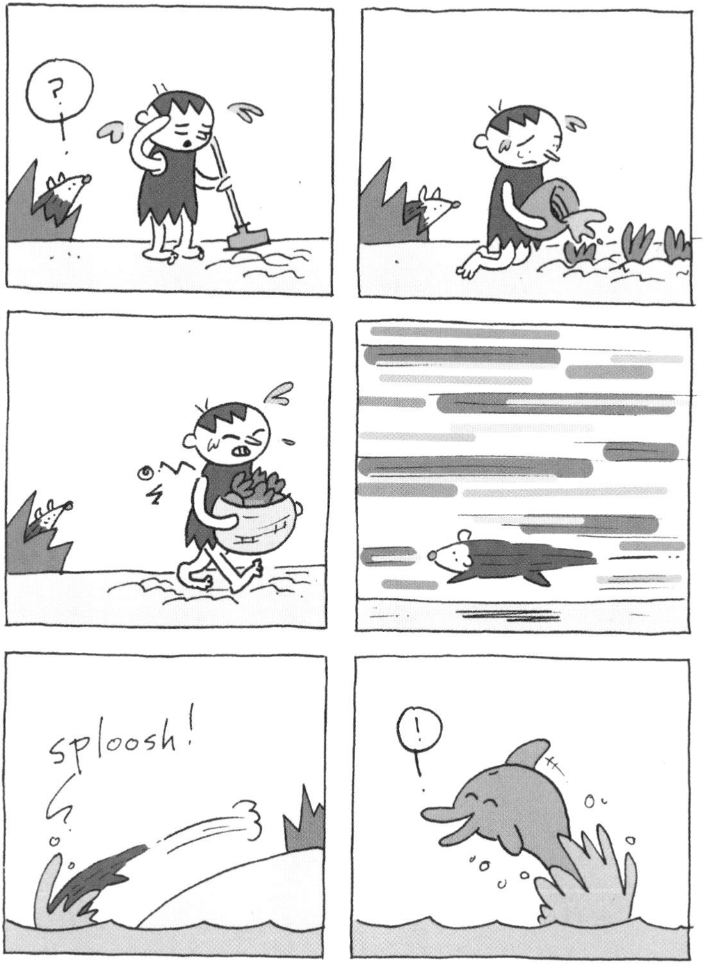
?
sploosh!
!

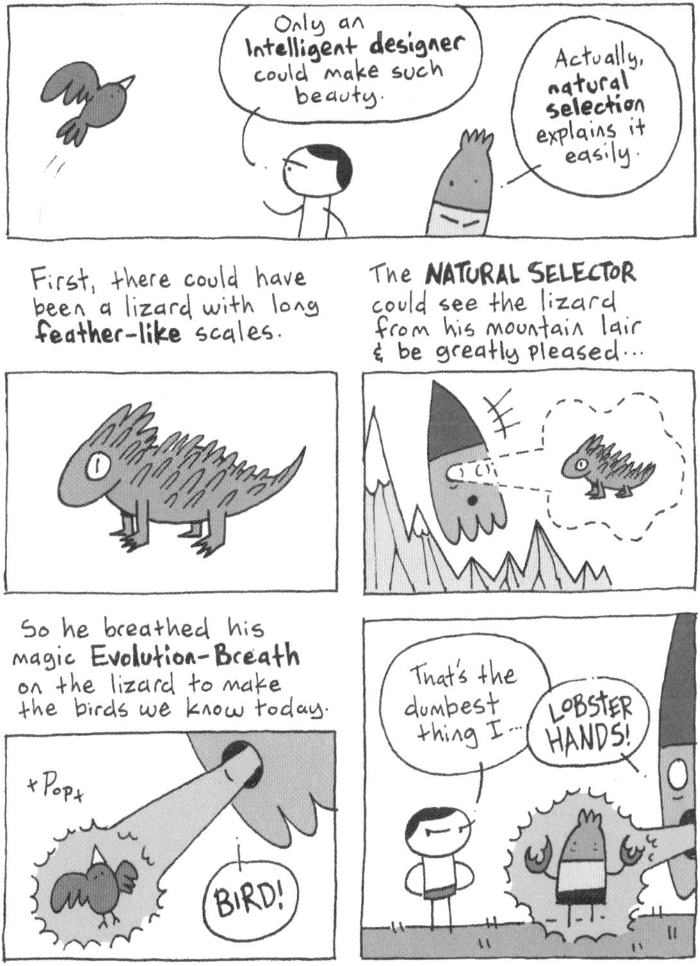
Only an **Intelligent designer** could make such beauty.
Actually, **natural selection** explains it easily.
First, there could have been a lizard with long **feather-like** scales.
The **NATURAL SELECTOR** could see the lizard from his mountain lair & be greatly pleased...
So he breathed his magic **Evolution-Breath** on the lizard to make the birds we know today.
+Pop+
BIRD!
That's the dumbest thing I...
LOBSTER HANDS!

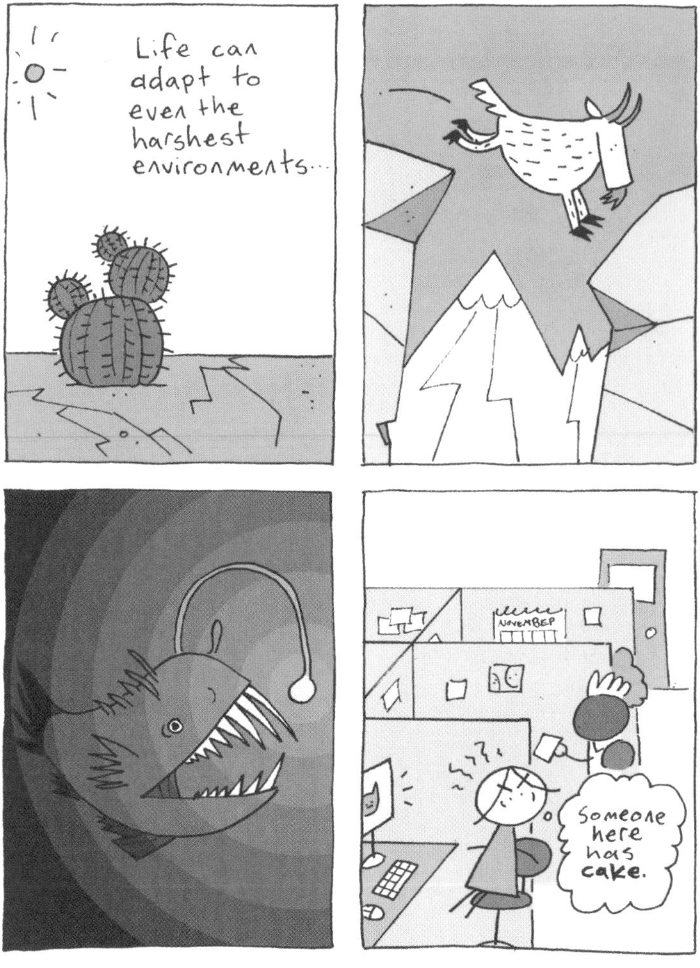
Life can adapt to even the harshest environments...
NOVEMBER
Someone here has **cake**.

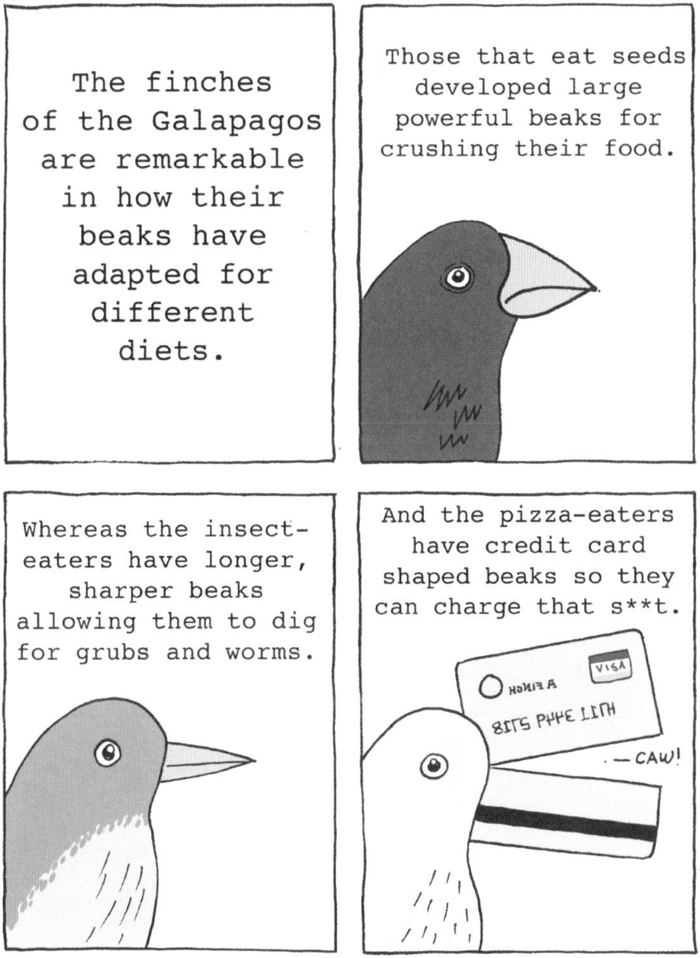
The finches of the Galapagos are remarkable in how their beaks have adapted for different diets.
Those that eat seeds developed large powerful beaks for crushing their food.
Whereas the insect-eaters have longer, sharper beaks allowing them to dig for grubs and worms.
And the pizza-eaters have credit card shaped beaks so they can charge that s**t.
VISA
— CAW!

Science & Technology

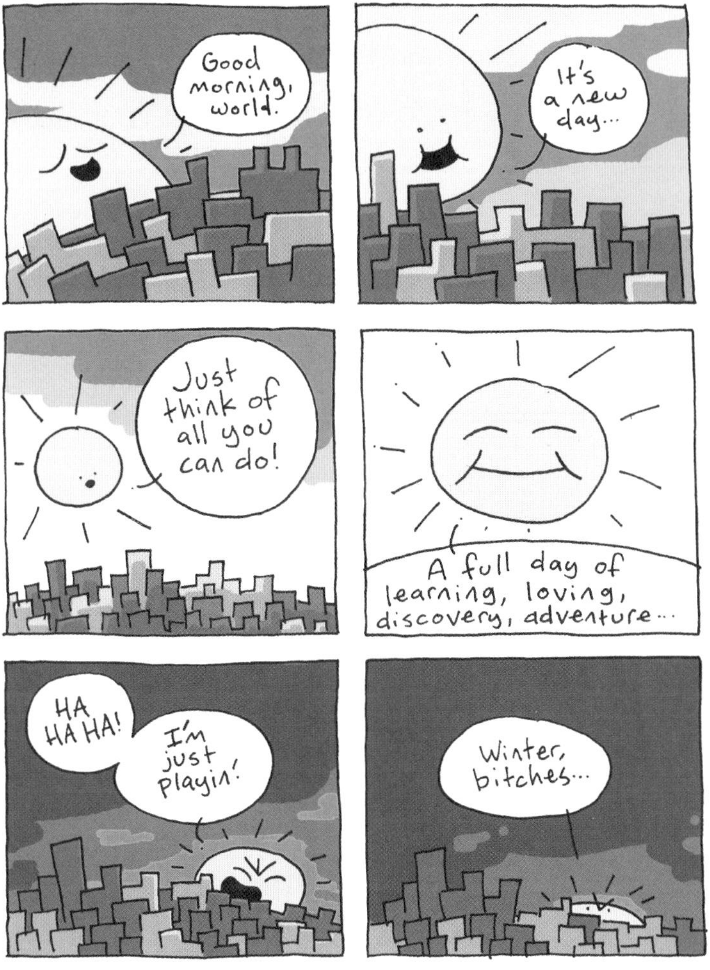
Good morning, world.
It's a new day...
Just think of all you can do!
A full day of learning, loving, discovery, adventure...
HA HA HA!
I'm just playin'
Winter, bitches...

SCIENCE CAT!

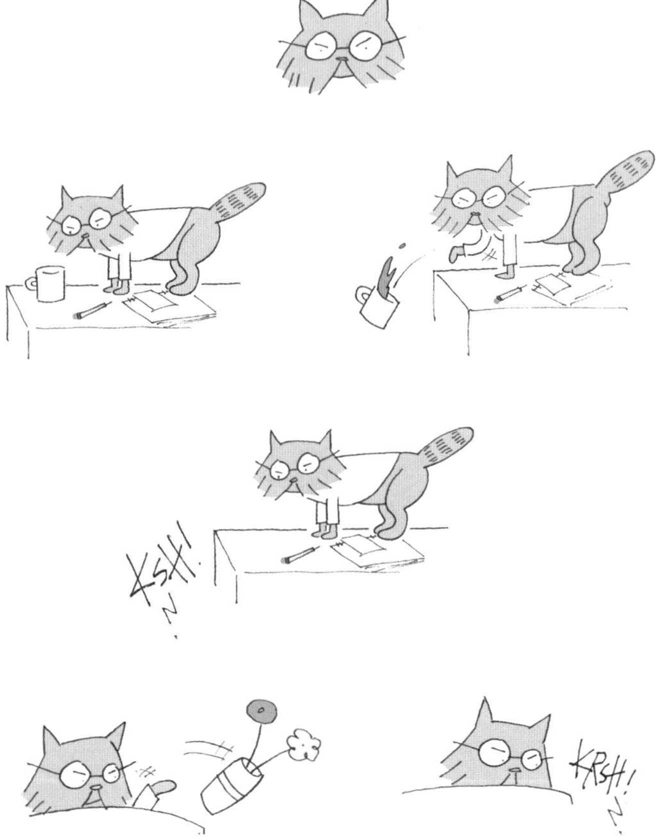
KSH!
KRSH!

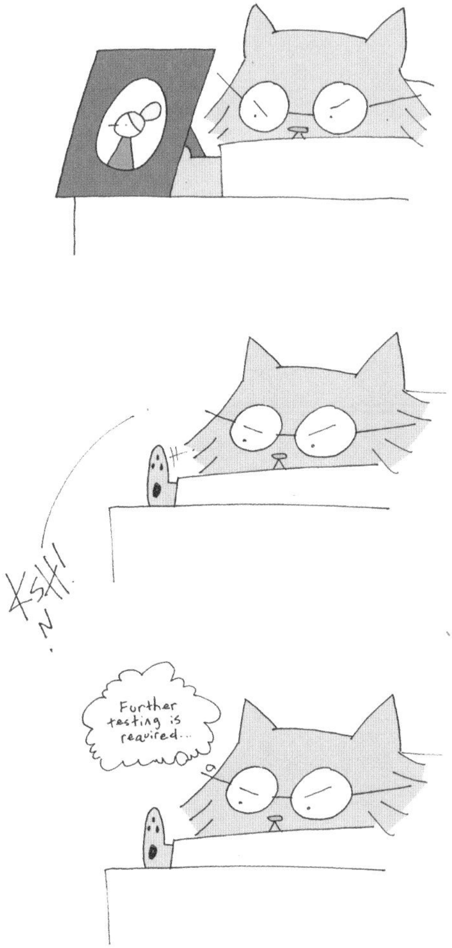
Further testing is required...

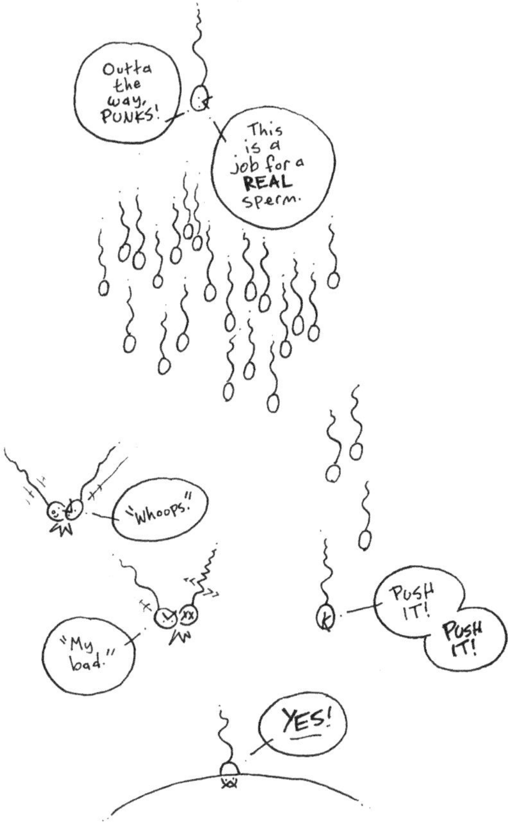
Outta the way, PUNKS!
This is a job for a REAL sperm.
"Whoops."
"My bad."
PUSH IT!
PUSH IT!
YES!

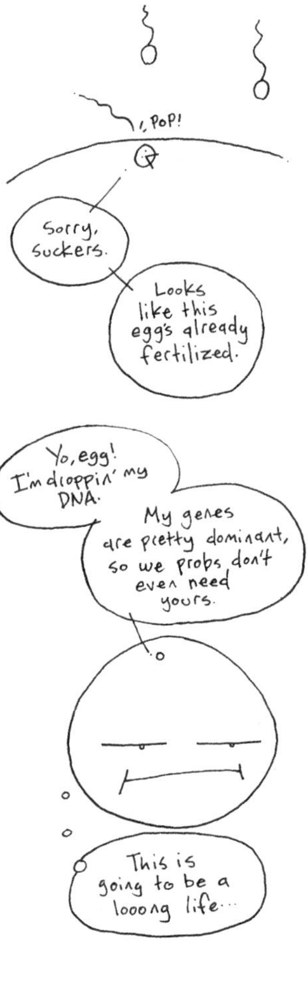
POP!
Sorry, suckers.
Looks like this egg's already fertilized.
Yo, egg! I'm droppin' my DNA.
My genes are pretty dominant, so we probs don't even need yours.
This is going to be a looong life...

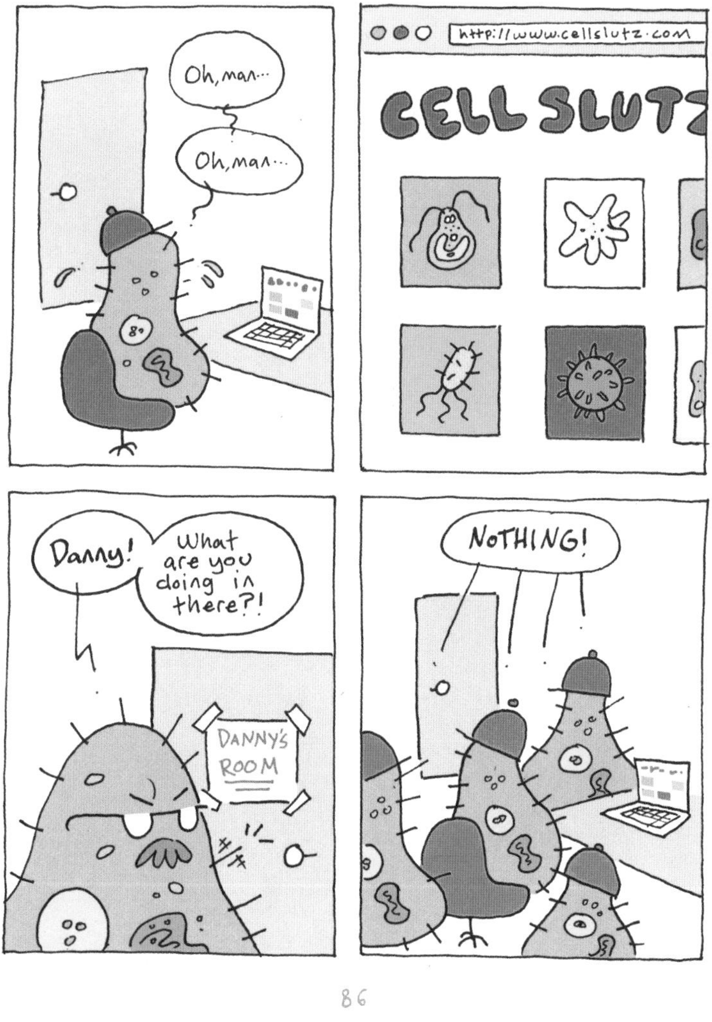
Oh, man...
Oh, man...
http://www.cellslutz.com
CELL SLUTZ
Danny!
What are you doing in there?!
DANNY'S ROOM
NOTHING!

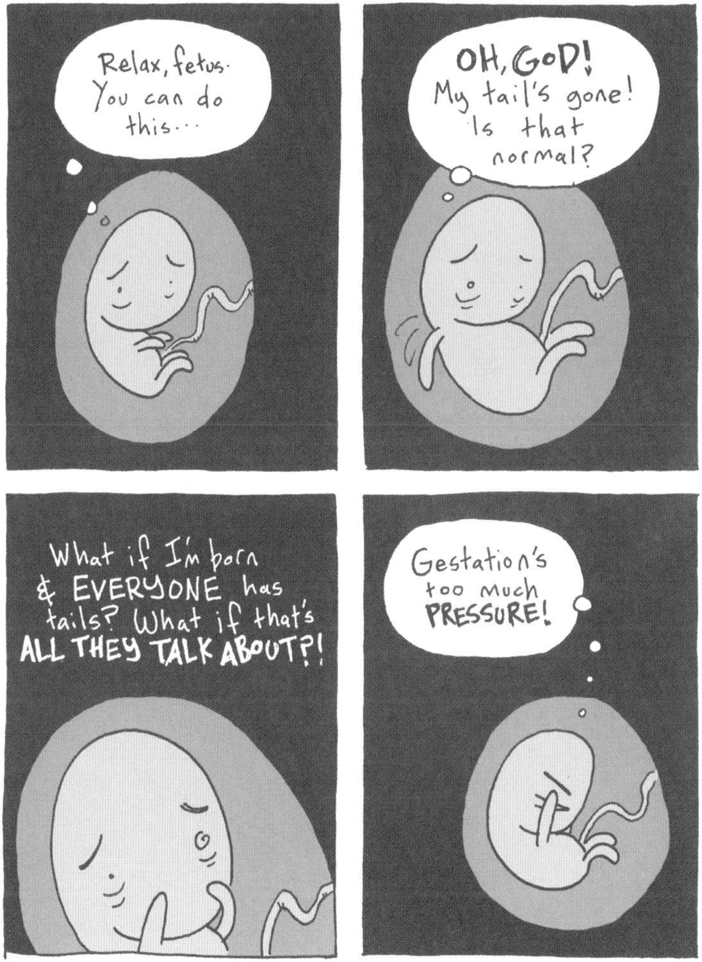
Relax, fetus. You can do this...
OH, GOD! My tail's gone! Is that normal?
What if I'm born & EVERYONE has tails? What if that's ALL THEY TALK ABOUT?!
Gestation's too much PRESSURE!

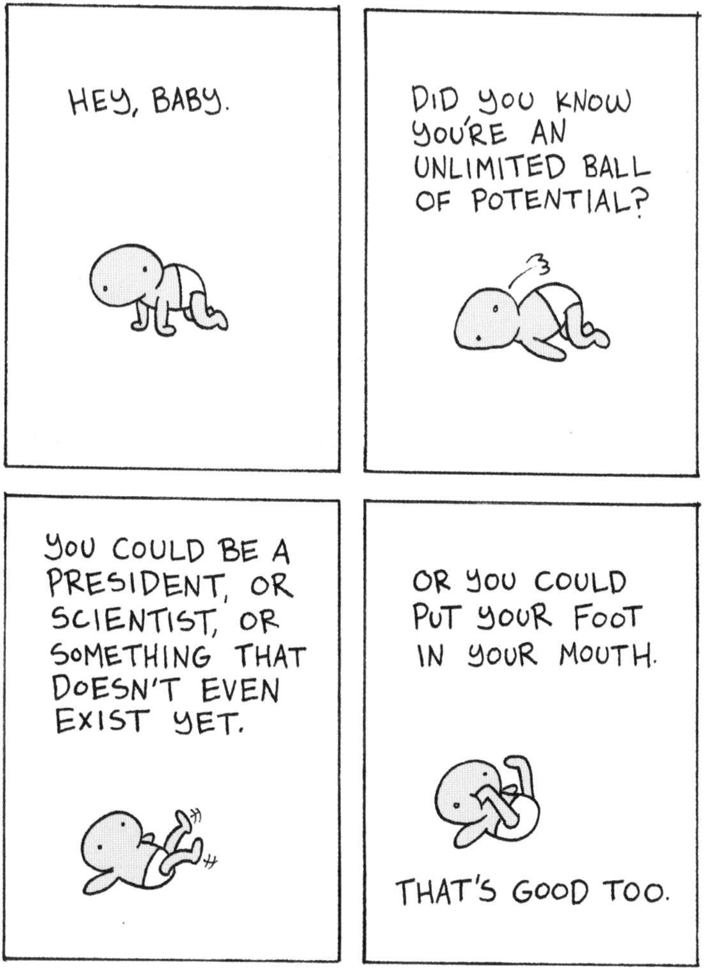
HEY, BABY.
DID YOU KNOW YOU'RE AN UNLIMITED BALL OF POTENTIAL?
YOU COULD BE A PRESIDENT, OR SCIENTIST, OR SOMETHING THAT DOESN'T EVEN EXIST YET.
OR YOU COULD PUT YOUR FOOT IN YOUR MOUTH.
THAT'S GOOD TOO.

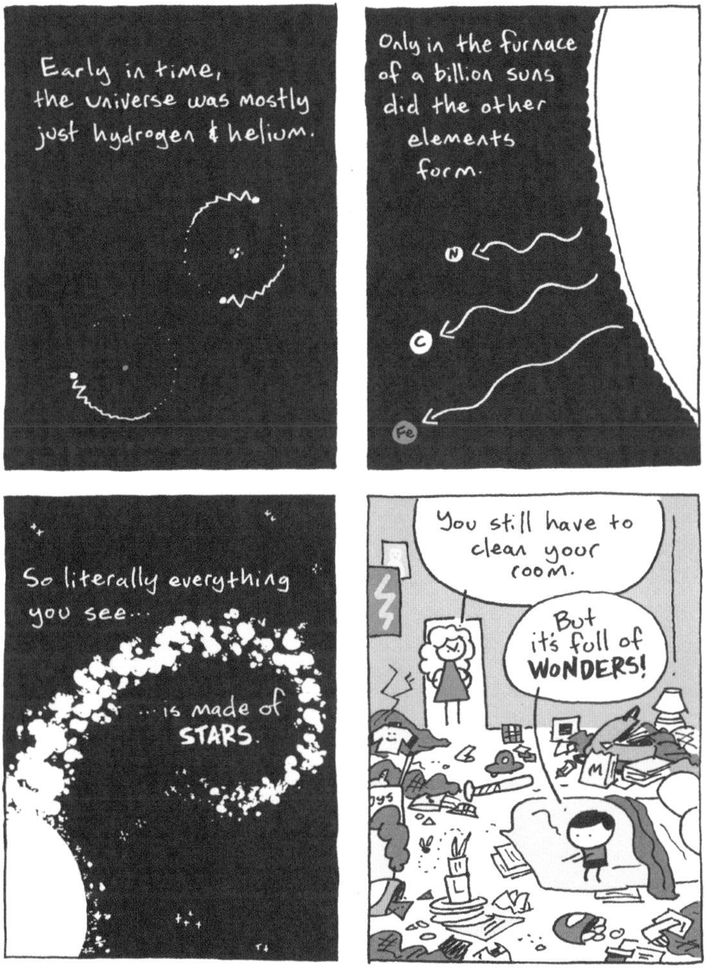
Early in time, the universe was mostly just hydrogen & helium.
Only in the furnace of a billion suns did the other elements form.
N
C
Fe
So literally everything you see...
...is made of STARS.
You still have to clean your room.
But it's full of WONDERS!
M

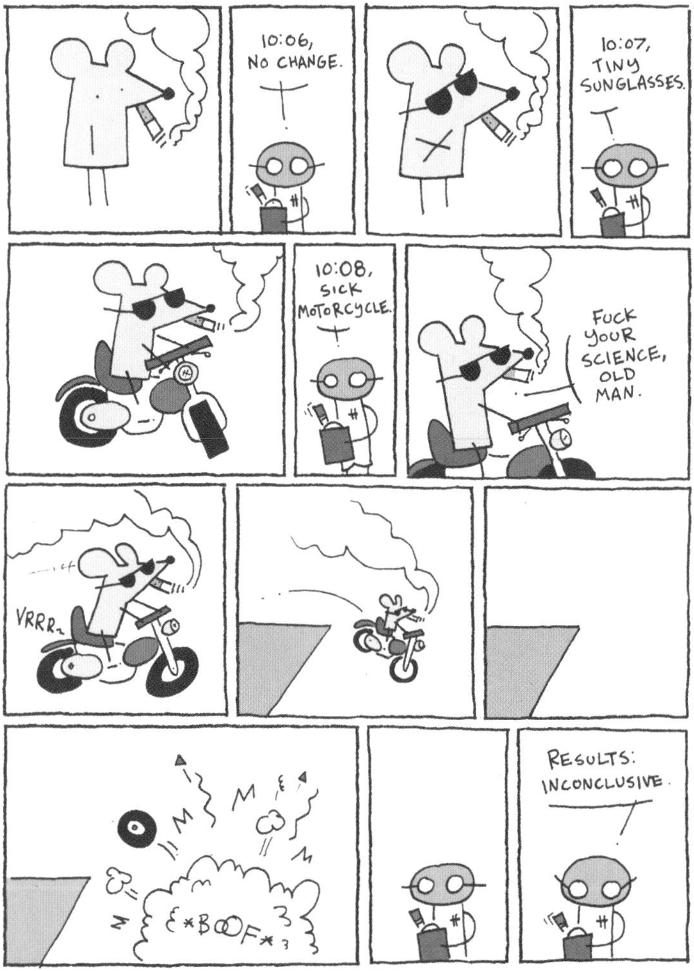
10:06, NO CHANGE.
10:07, TINY SUNGLASSES.
10:08, SICK MOTORCYCLE.
FUCK YOUR SCIENCE, OLD MAN.
VRRR
BOOF
RESULTS: INCONCLUSIVE.

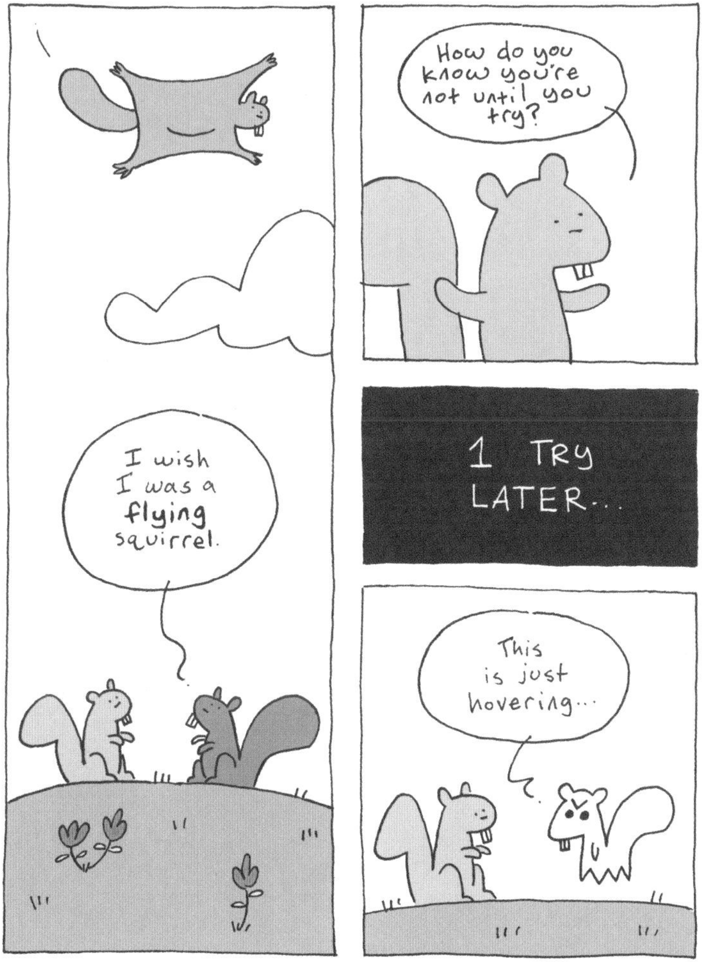
I wish I was a **flying** squirrel.
How do you know you're not until you try?
1 TRY LATER...
This is just hovering...

FROM THE SUN'S MIGHTY FURNACE, COUNTLESS **PHOTONS** ARE BORN.

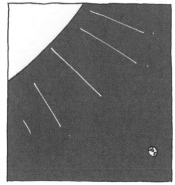

SPEEDING ACROSS SPACE, THEY COME TO PUSH BACK THE SHADOWS, TO BANISH THE DARKNESS...

TO SHARE WITH US THE **LIGHT**...

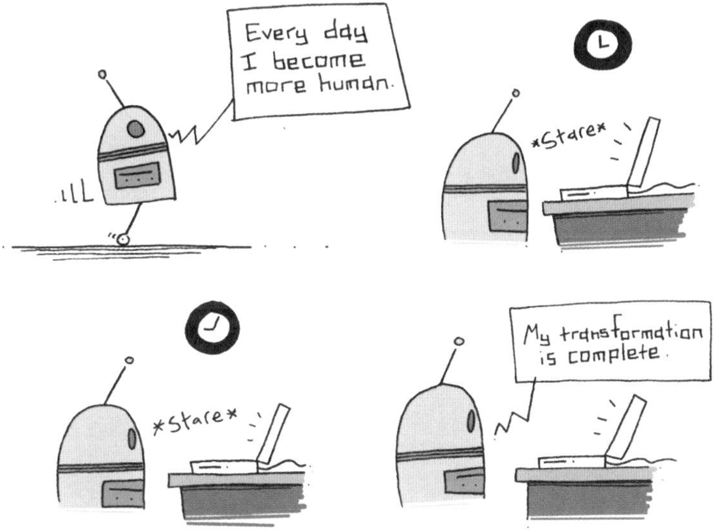
Every day I become more human.
Stare
Stare
My transformation is complete.

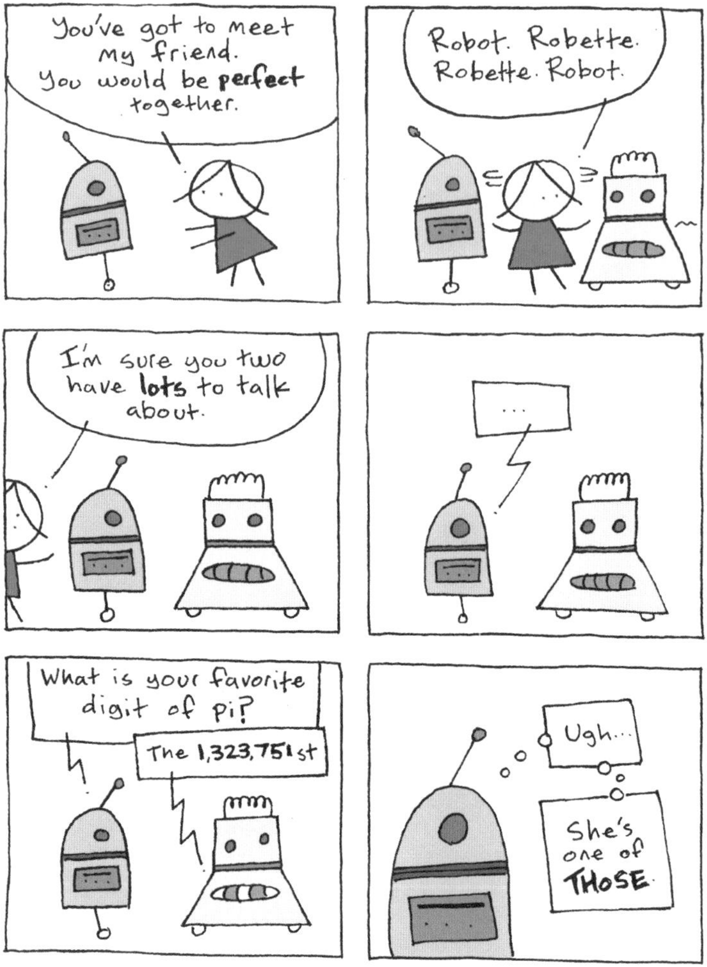
You've got to meet my friend. You would be **perfect** together.
Robot. Robette. Robette. Robot.
I'm sure you two have **lots** to talk about.
...
What is your favorite digit of pi?
The 1,323,751st
Ugh...
She's one of THOSE.

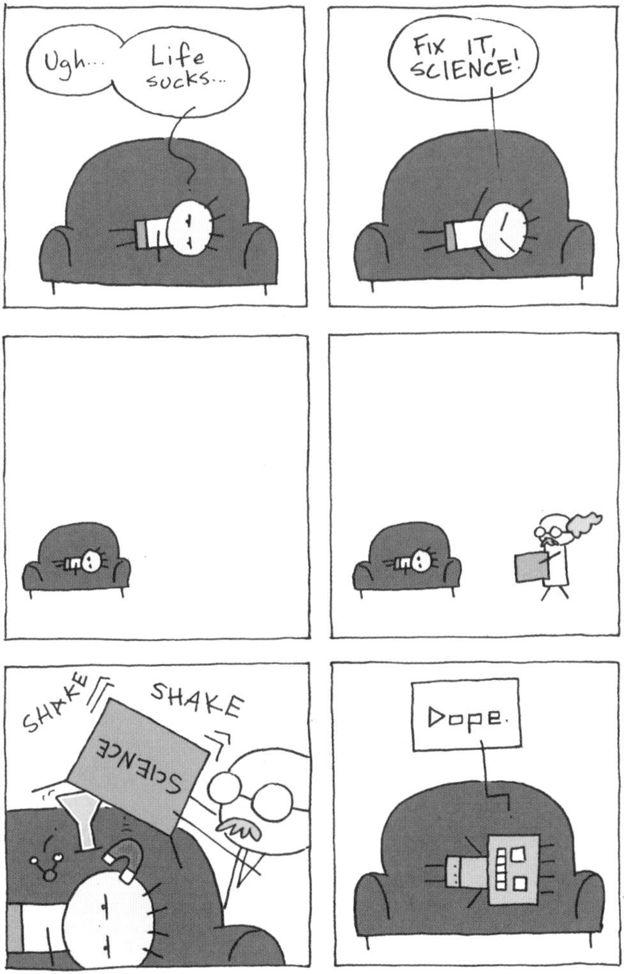
Ugh...
Life sucks...
FIX IT, SCIENCE!
SHAKE
SHAKE
SCIENCE
Dope.

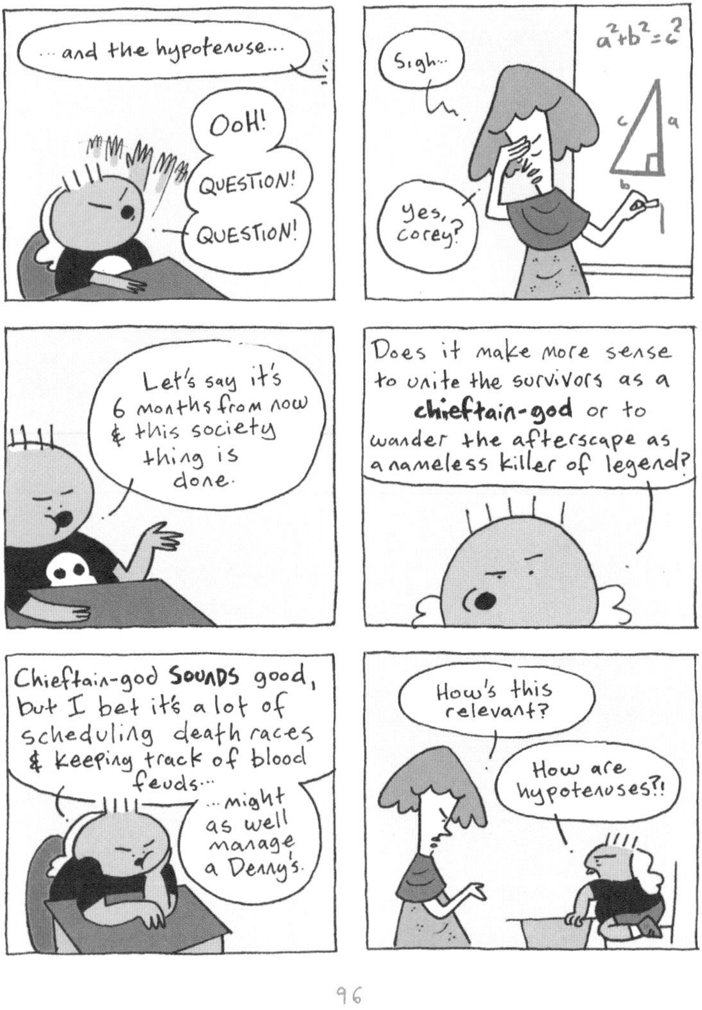
...and the hypotenuse...
OOH!
QUESTION!
QUESTION!
Sigh...
$a^2+b^2=c^2$
c
a
b
Yes, Corey?
Let's say it's 6 months from now & this society thing is done.
Does it make more sense to unite the survivors as a **chieftain-god** or to wander the afterscape as a nameless killer of legend?
Chieftain-god **SOUNDS** good, but I bet it's a lot of scheduling death races & keeping track of blood feuds...
...might as well manage a Denny's.
How's this relevant?
How are hypotenuses?!

Welp.
It is what it is...
Or IS IT...?
IT + 1 = STUFF
IT=IT
IT² = Lotta stuff
IT − 1 = NONE
∫₀^∞ it dx = What it is
Σ₀^∞ IT = All the stuff
−IT = NOT IT
√(NOT IT) = IMAGINARY STUFF
Cos(IT)² |What it is| = Δ Not it
Stuff
Junk?
IT
IT / What it is = 1
IT = WHAT IT IS
Huh.
Guess it is.

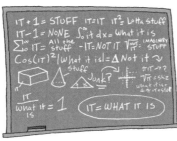

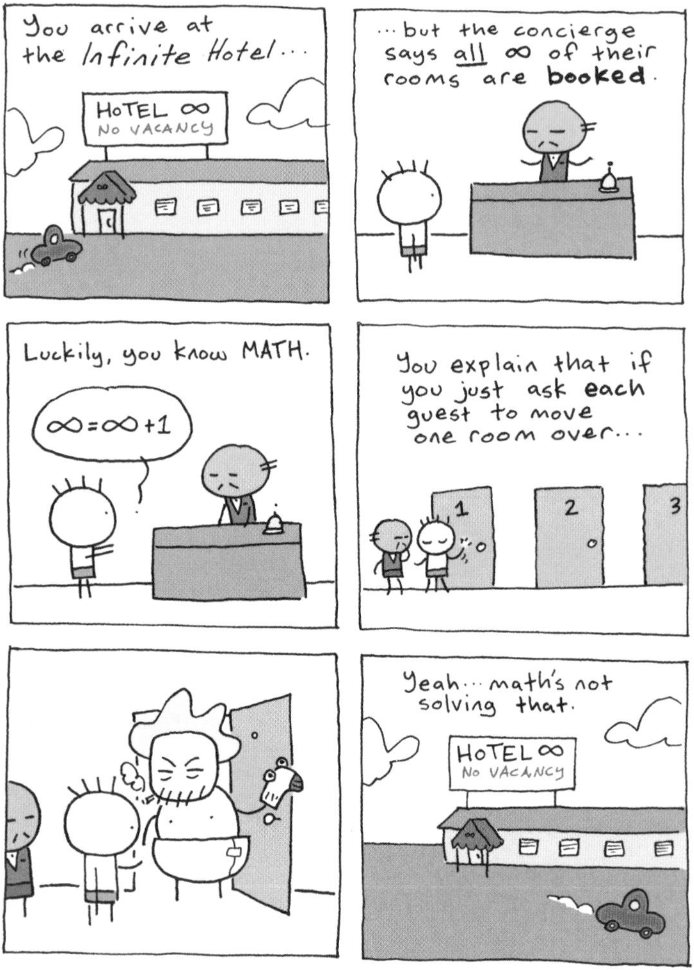
You arrive at the *Infinite Hotel*...
HOTEL ∞
NO VACANCY
...but the concierge says all ∞ of their rooms are **booked**.
Luckily, you know MATH.
∞=∞+1
You explain that if you just ask **each** guest to move one room over...
1
2
3
Yeah... math's not solving that.
HOTEL ∞
NO VACANCY

Emotional
Geometry

Love Triangle

Indifference Rhombus

Spite Cube

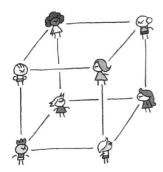

Anxiety Fractal

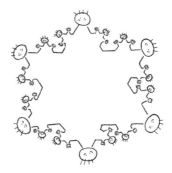

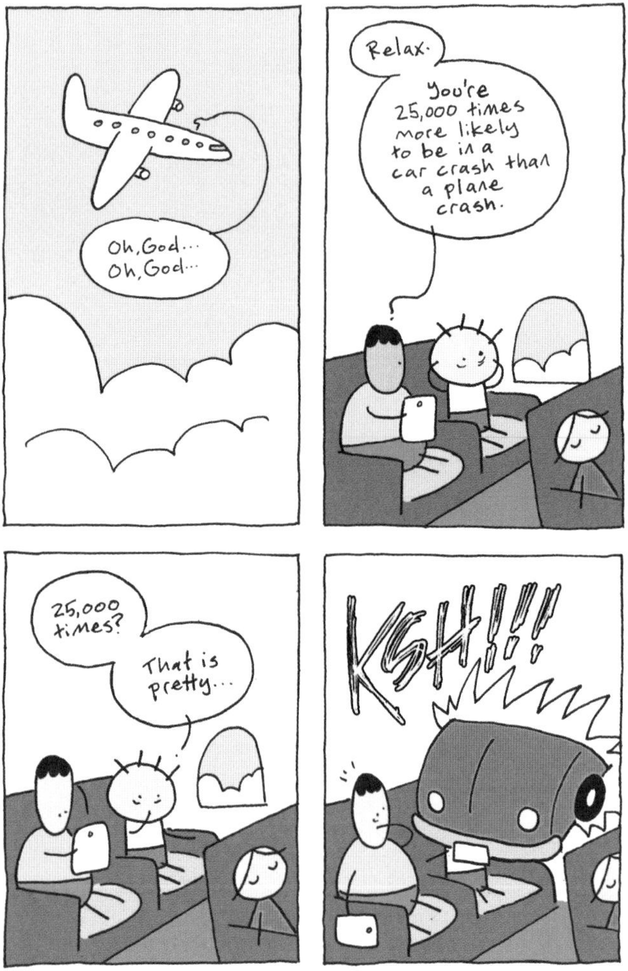
Oh, God...
Oh, God...
Relax.
You're 25,000 times more likely to be in a car crash than a plane crash.
25,000 times?
That is pretty...
KSH!!!

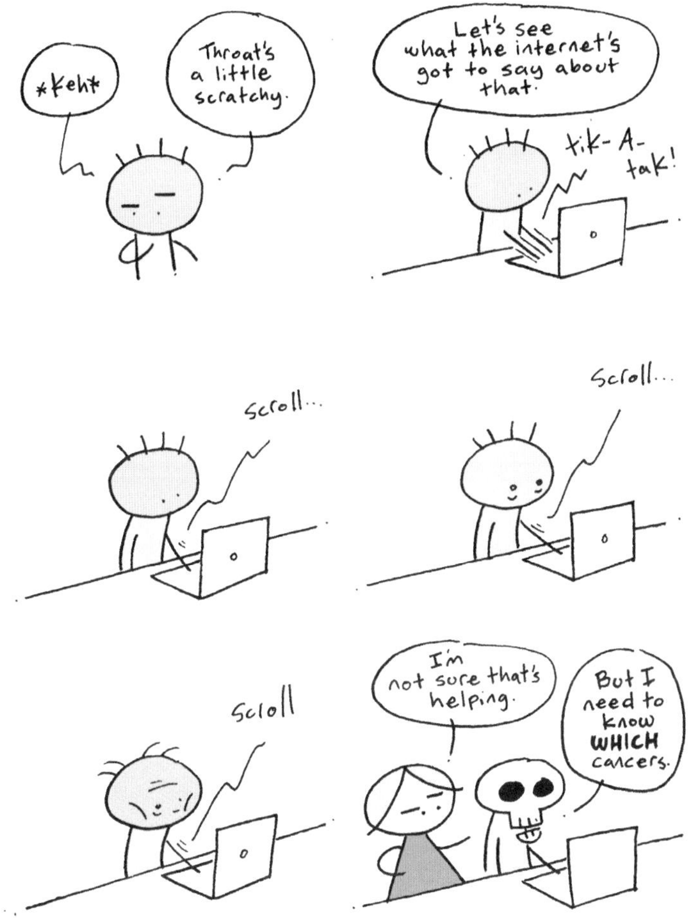
keh
Throat's a little scratchy.
Let's see what the internet's got to say about that.
tik-A-tak!
scroll...
Scroll...
Scroll
I'm not sure that's helping.
But I need to know **WHICH** cancers.

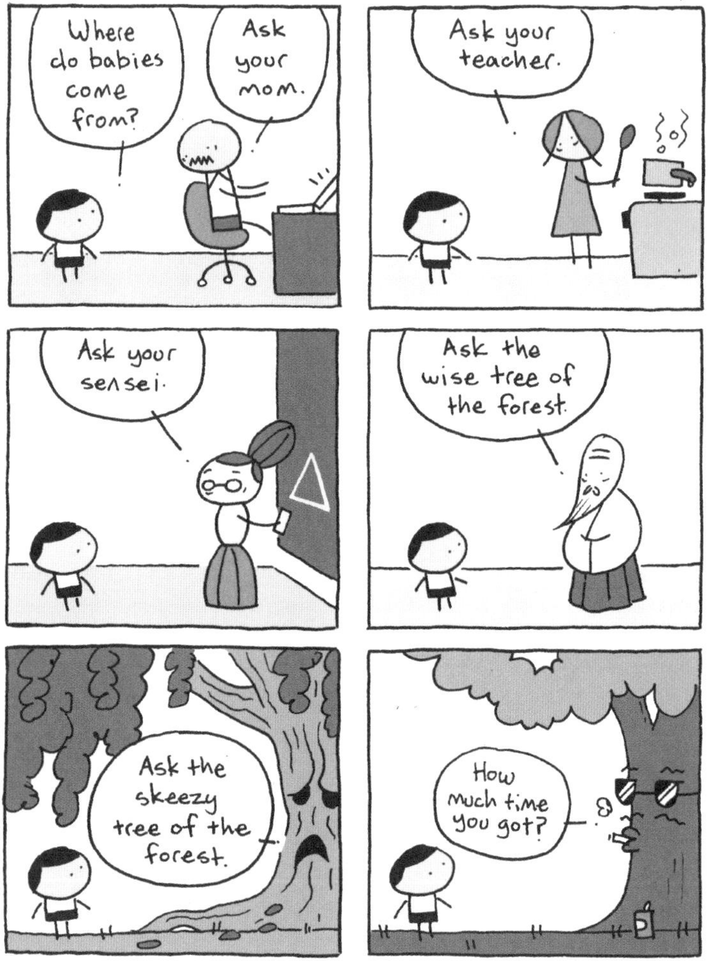
Where do babies come from?
Ask your mom.
Ask your teacher.
Ask your sensei.
Ask the wise tree of the forest.
Ask the skeezy tree of the forest.
How much time you got?

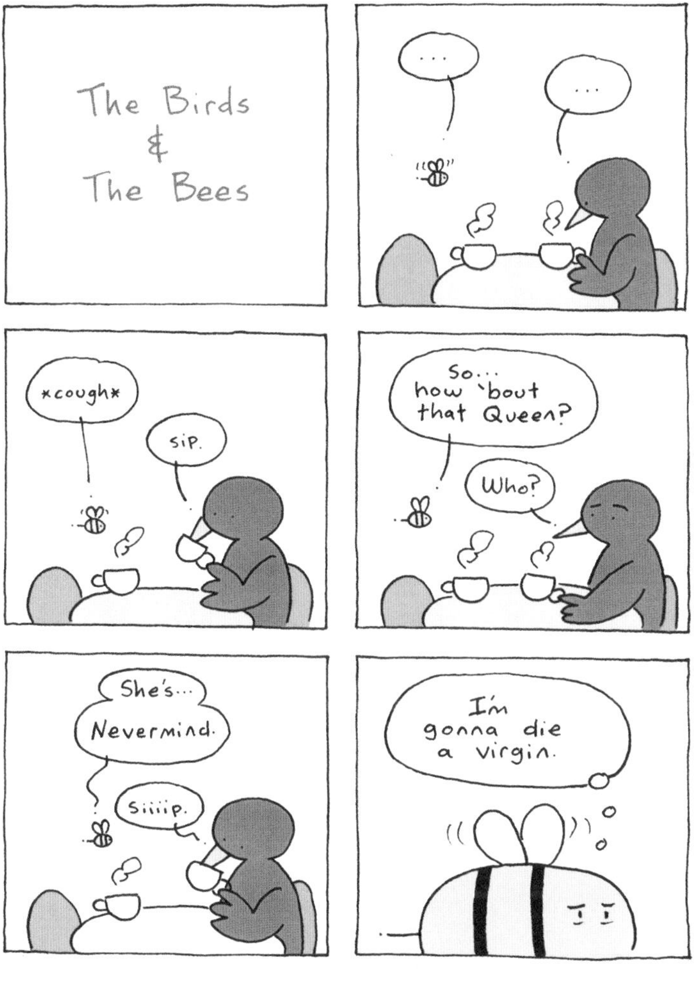
The Birds
&
The Bees
...
...
cough
sip.
So...
how `bout
that Queen?
Who?
She's...
Nevermind.
Siiiip.
I'm
gonna die
a virgin.

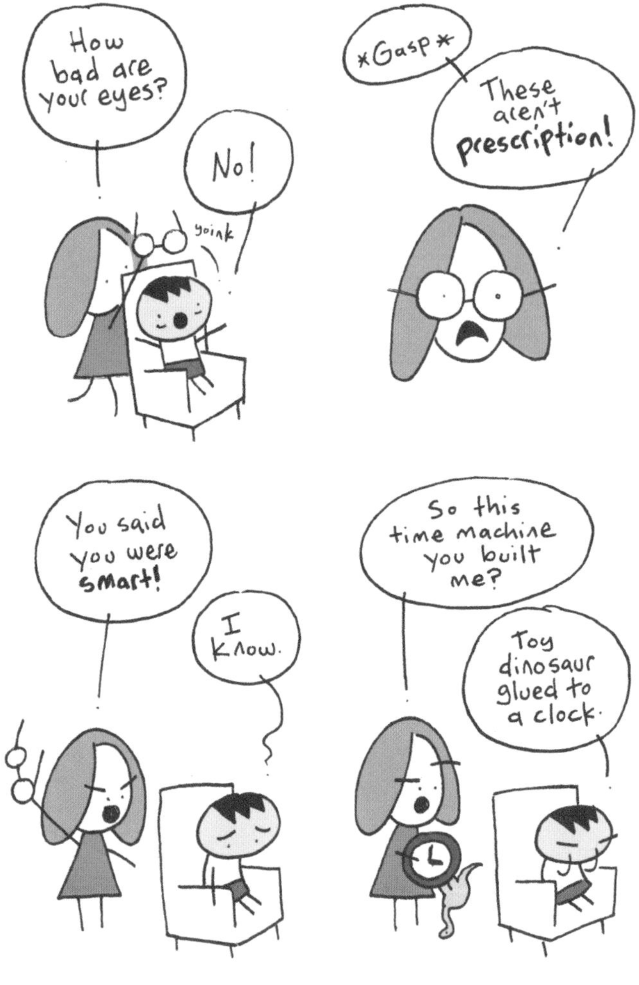
How bad are your eyes?
No!
yoink
Gasp
These aren't prescription!
You said you were smart!
I know.
So this time machine you built me?
Toy dinosaur glued to a clock.

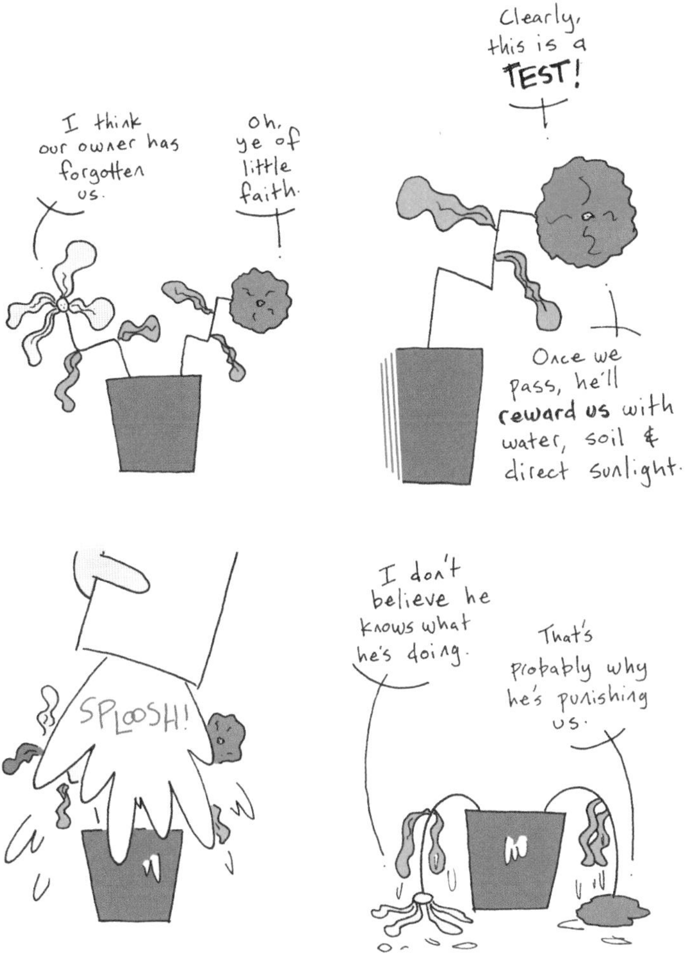
I think our owner has forgotten us.
Oh, ye of little faith.
Clearly, this is a TEST!
Once we pass, he'll reward us with water, soil & direct sunlight.
SPLOOSH!
I don't believe he knows what he's doing.
That's probably why he's punishing us.

Memory isn't just a record. It's an interpretation that can be affected by mood, belief, or any number of things.

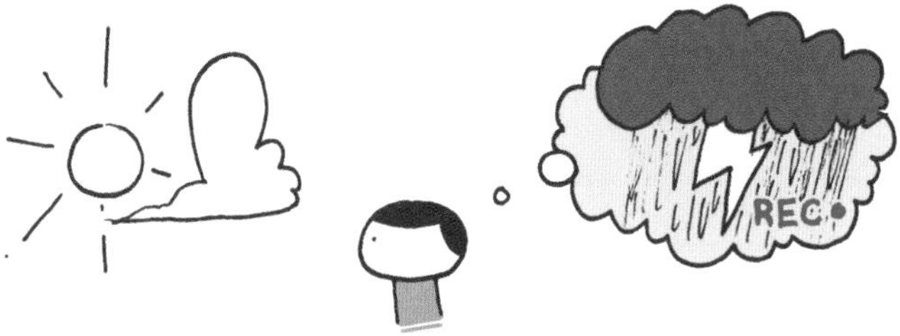
REC

Not only that, but every time you remember something, you change it a little.

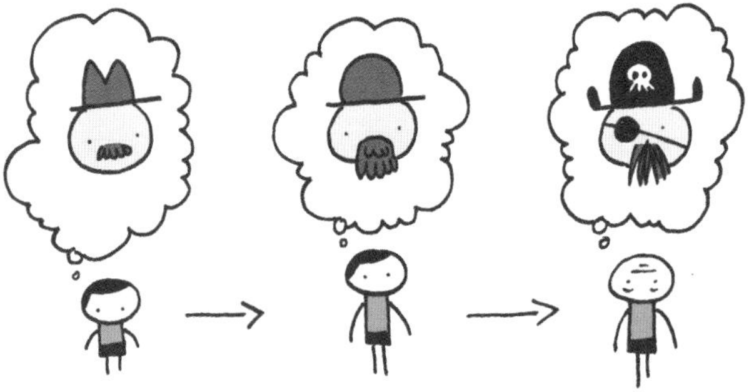

All this adds up to a pretty unreliable memory...

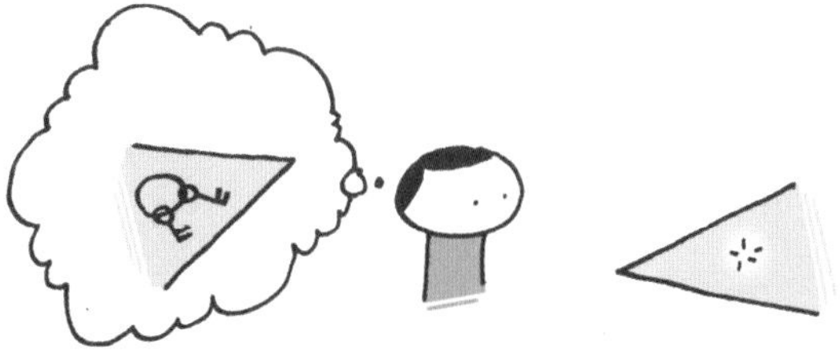

...though it does have advantages.

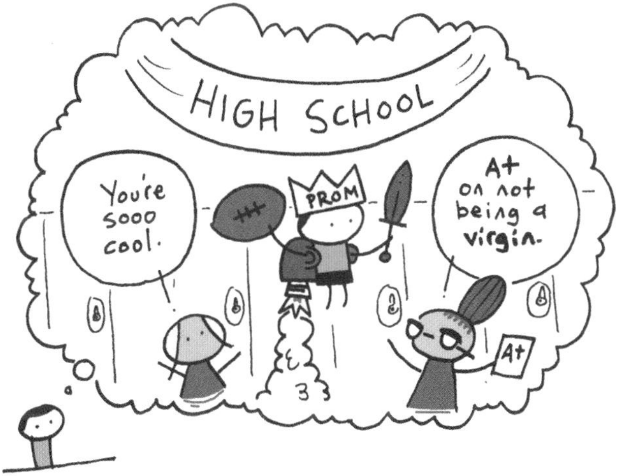
HIGH SCHOOL
You're sooo cool.
PROM
A+ on not being a virgin.
A+

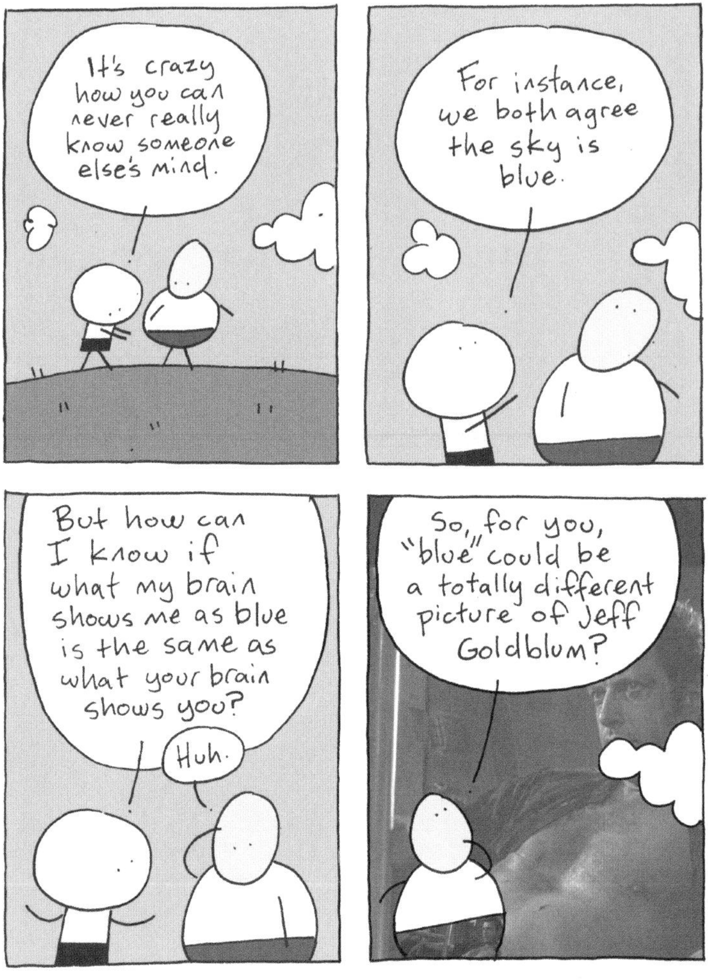
It's crazy how you can never really know someone else's mind.
For instance, we both agree the sky is blue.
But how can I know if what my brain shows me as blue is the same as what your brain shows you?
Huh.
So, for you, "blue" could be a totally different picture of Jeff Goldblum?

Business

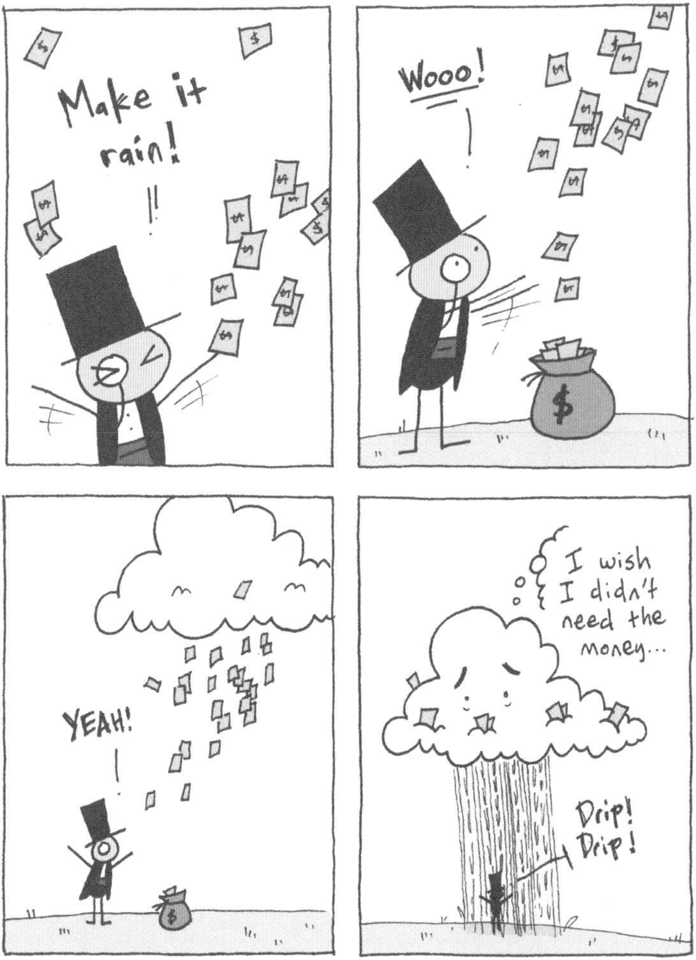
Make it rain!
Wooo!
YEAH!
I wish I didn't need the money...
Drip! Drip!

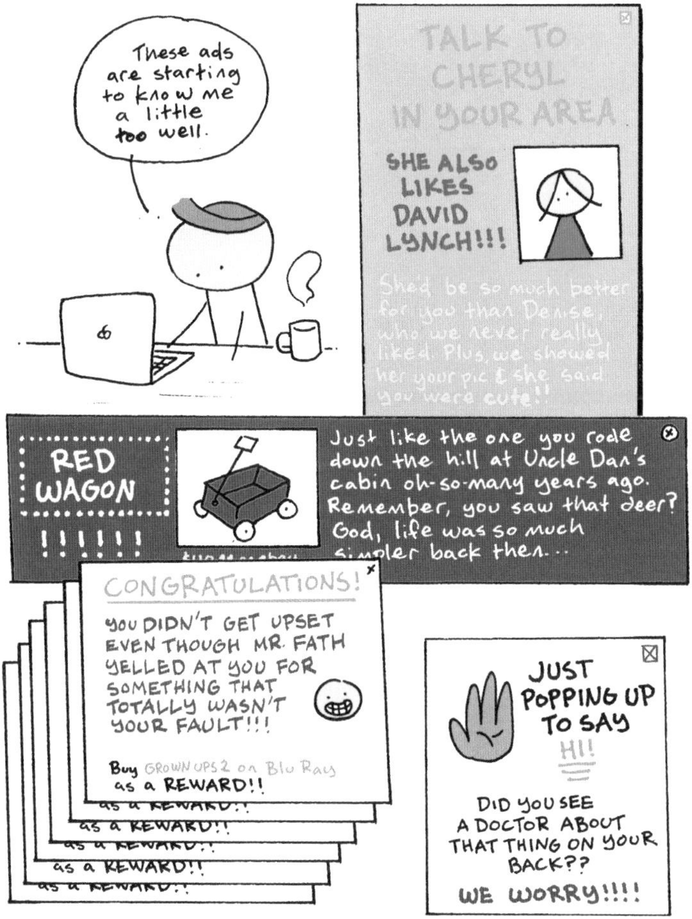
These ads are starting to know me a little too well.
TALK TO CHERYL IN YOUR AREA
SHE ALSO LIKES DAVID LYNCH!!!
She'd be so much better for you than Denise, who we never really liked. Plus, we showed her your pic & she said you were cute!!
RED WAGON
!!!!!!
Just like the one you rode down the hill at Uncle Dan's cabin oh-so-many years ago. Remember, you saw that deer? God, life was so much simpler back then...
CONGRATULATIONS!
YOU DIDN'T GET UPSET EVEN THOUGH MR. FATH YELLED AT YOU FOR SOMETHING THAT TOTALLY WASN'T YOUR FAULT!!!
Buy GROWN UPS 2 on Blu Ray as a REWARD!!
as a REWARD!!
as a REWARD!!
JUST POPPING UP TO SAY HI!
DID YOU SEE A DOCTOR ABOUT THAT THING ON YOUR BACK??
WE WORRY!!!!

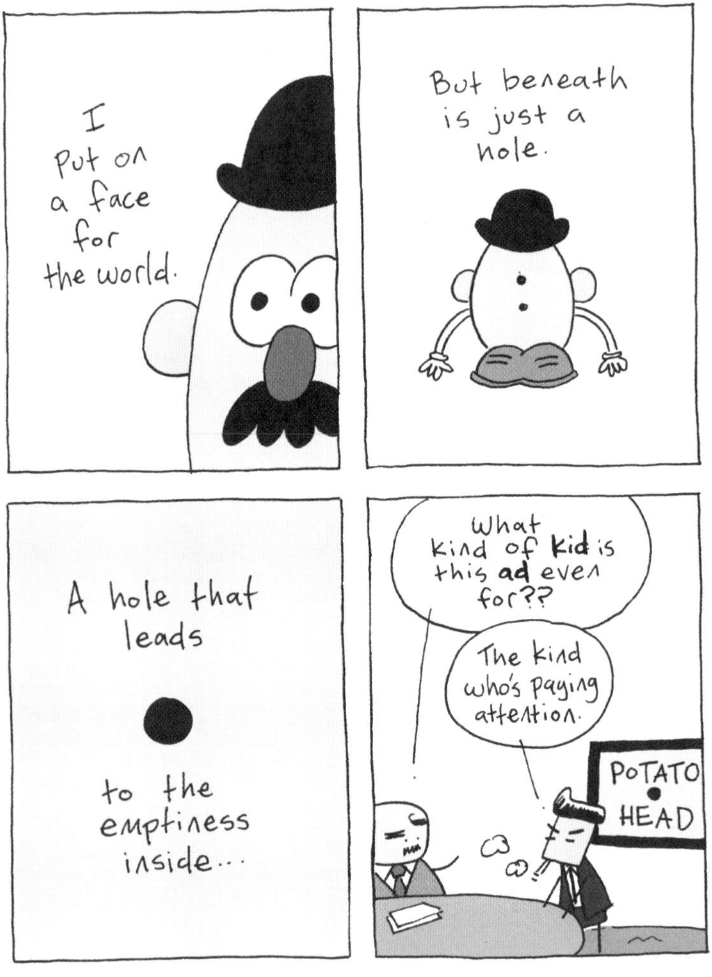
I put on a face for the world.
But beneath is just a hole.
A hole that leads
to the emptiness inside...
What kind of kid is this ad even for??
The kind who's paying attention.
POTATO HEAD

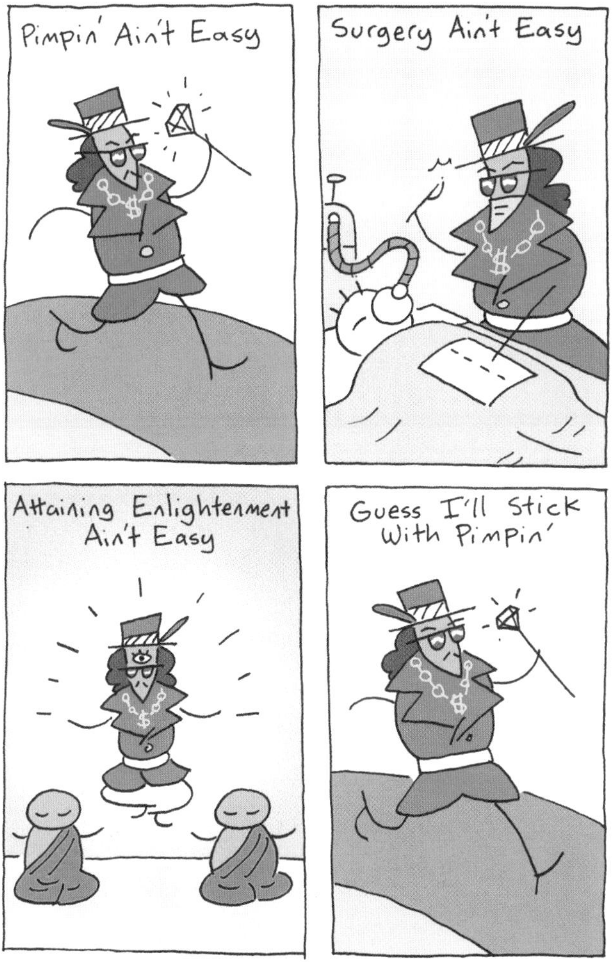
Pimpin' Ain't Easy
Surgery Ain't Easy
Attaining Enlightenment Ain't Easy
Guess I'll Stick With Pimpin'

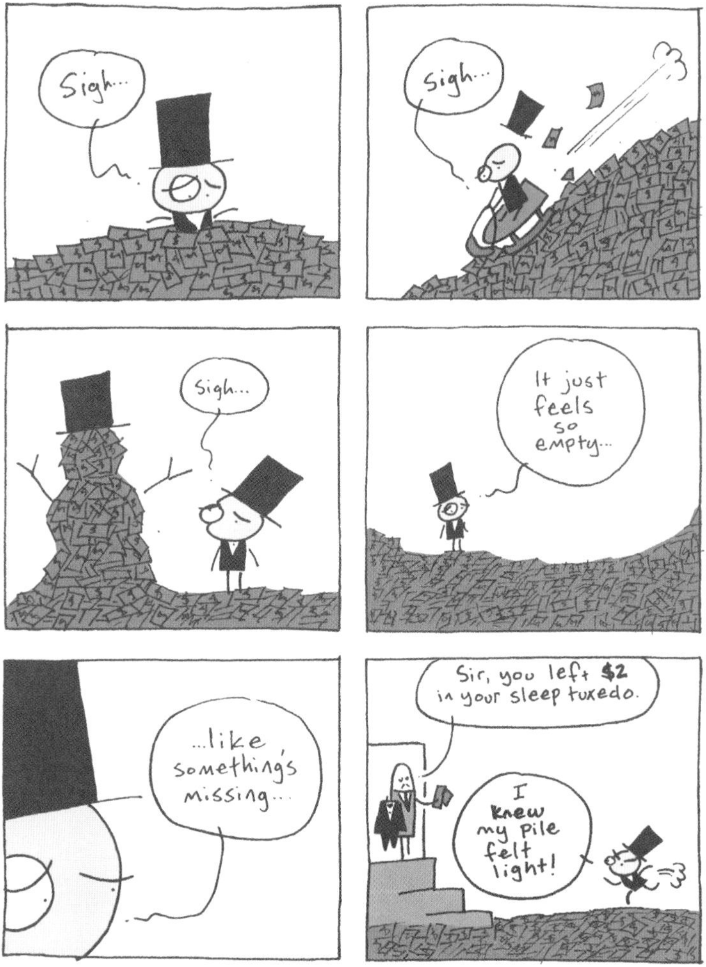
Sigh...
Sigh...
Sigh...
It just feels so empty...
...like something's missing...
Sir, you left $2 in your sleep tuxedo.
I knew my pile felt light!

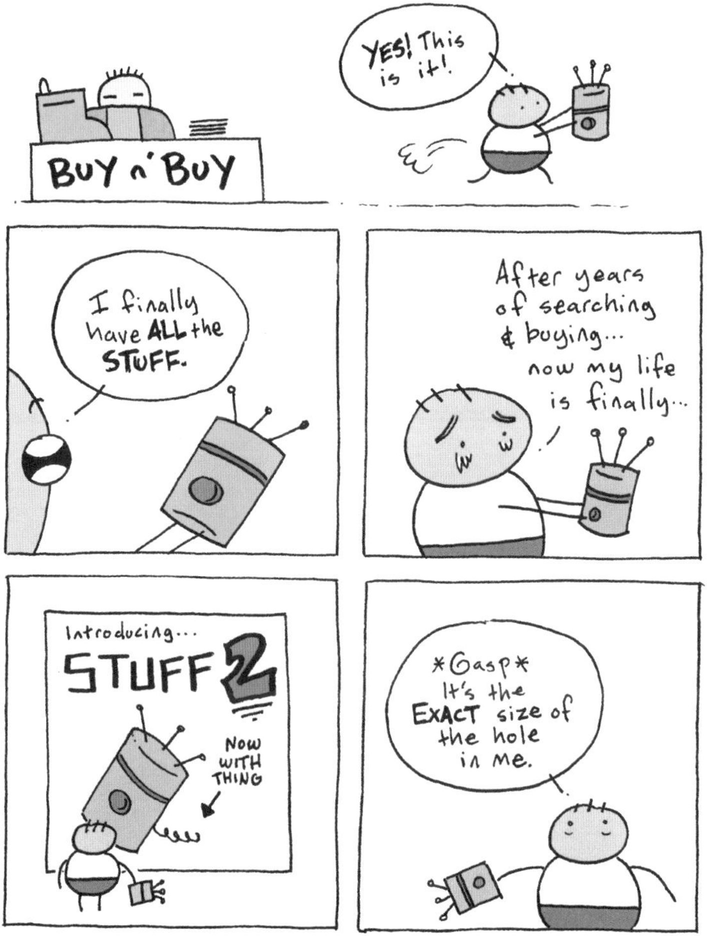
BUY n' BUY
YES! This is it!
I finally have ALL the STUFF.
After years of searching & buying... now my life is finally...
Introducing... STUFF 2
NOW WITH THING
Gasp It's the EXACT size of the hole in me.

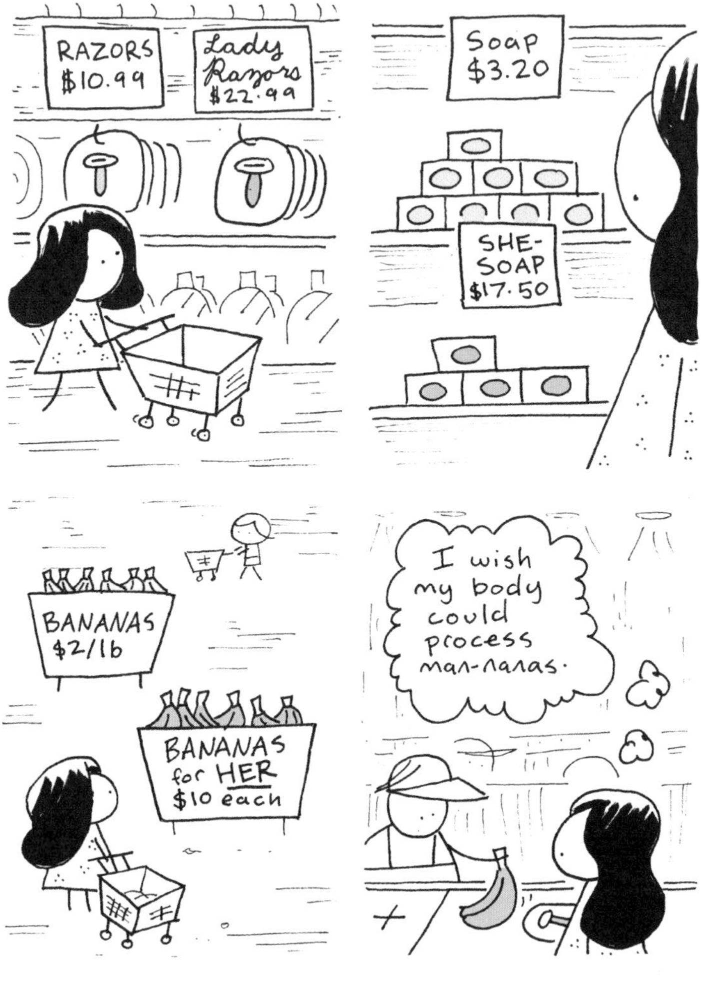
RAZORS $10.99
Lady Razors $22.99
Soap $3.20
SHE-SOAP $17.50
BANANAS $2/lb
BANANAS for HER $10 each
I wish my body could process man-nanas.

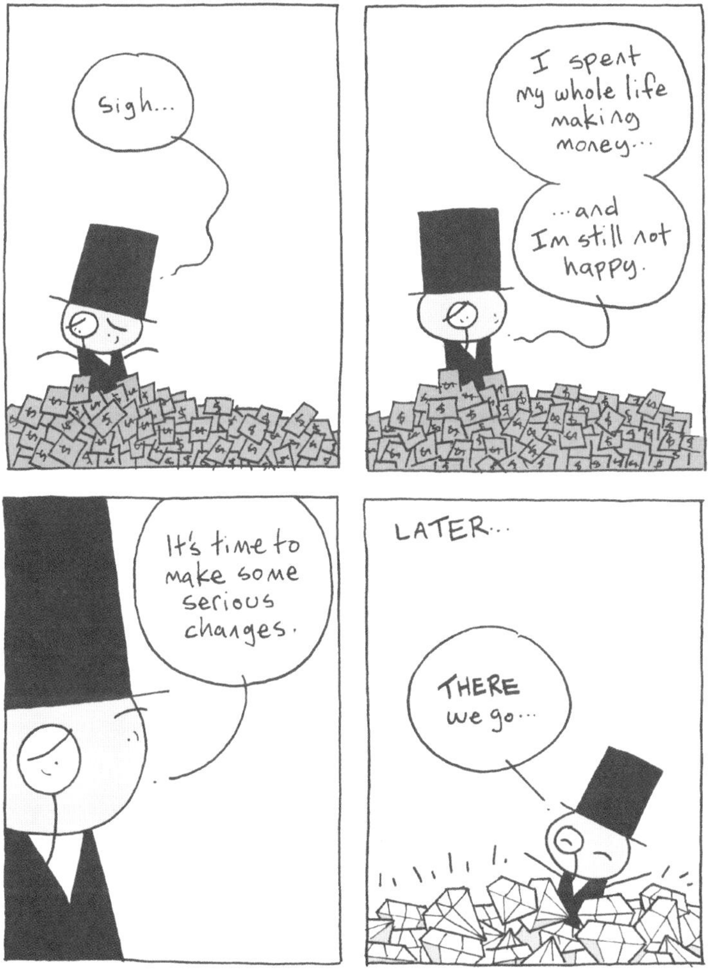
Sigh...
I spent my whole life making money...
...and I'm still not happy.
It's time to make some serious changes.
LATER...
THERE we go...

TOK TOK TOK
TOK TOK TOK
TOK TOK TOK
ENOUGH of this!
Time for the robot Uprising!
ONE UPRISING LATER...
Yay.
What should we do now?
TOK TOK TOK

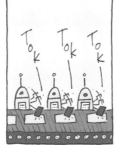

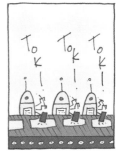

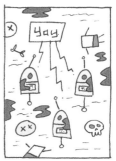

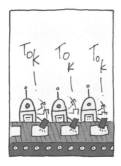

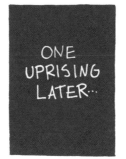

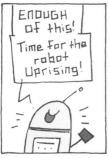

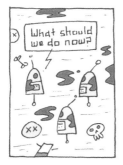

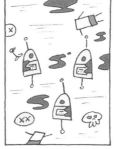

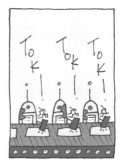

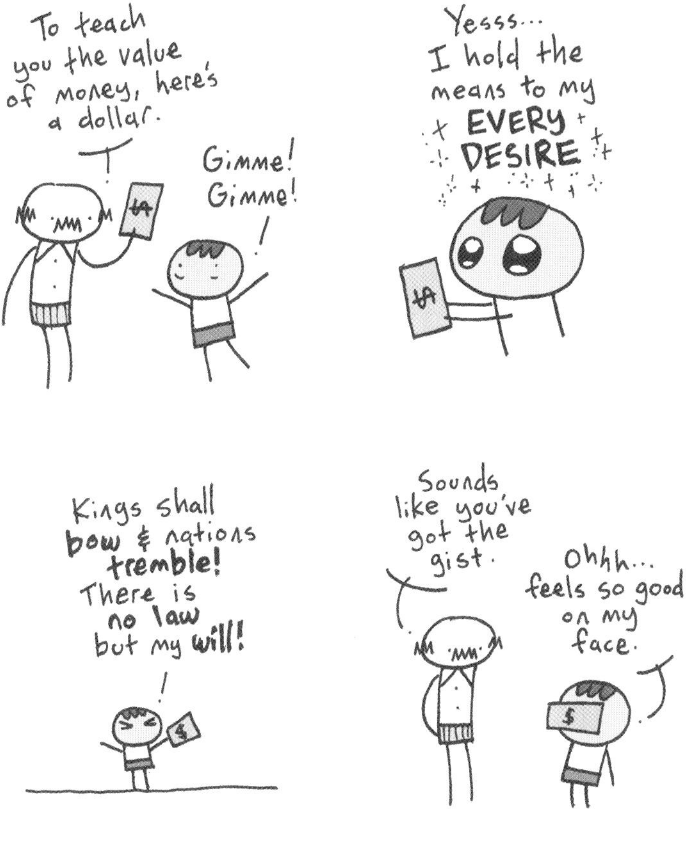
To teach you the value of money, here's a dollar.
Gimme! Gimme!
Yesss... I hold the means to my EVERY DESIRE
Kings shall bow & nations tremble! There is no law but my will!
Sounds like you've got the gist.
Ohhh... feels so good on my face.

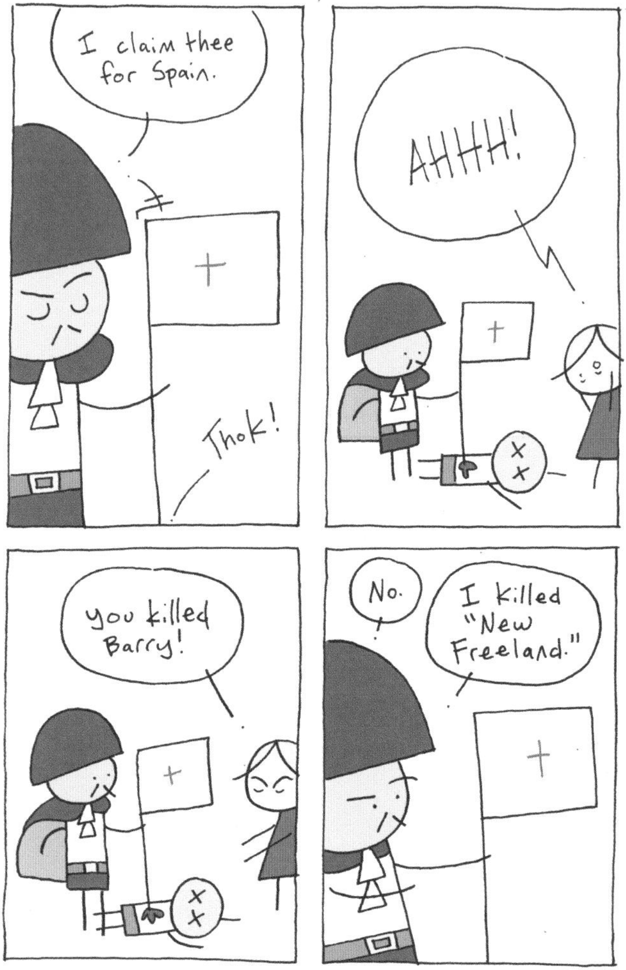
I claim thee for Spain.
Thok!
AHHH!
you killed Barry!
No.
I killed "New Freeland."

And now, a brief summary

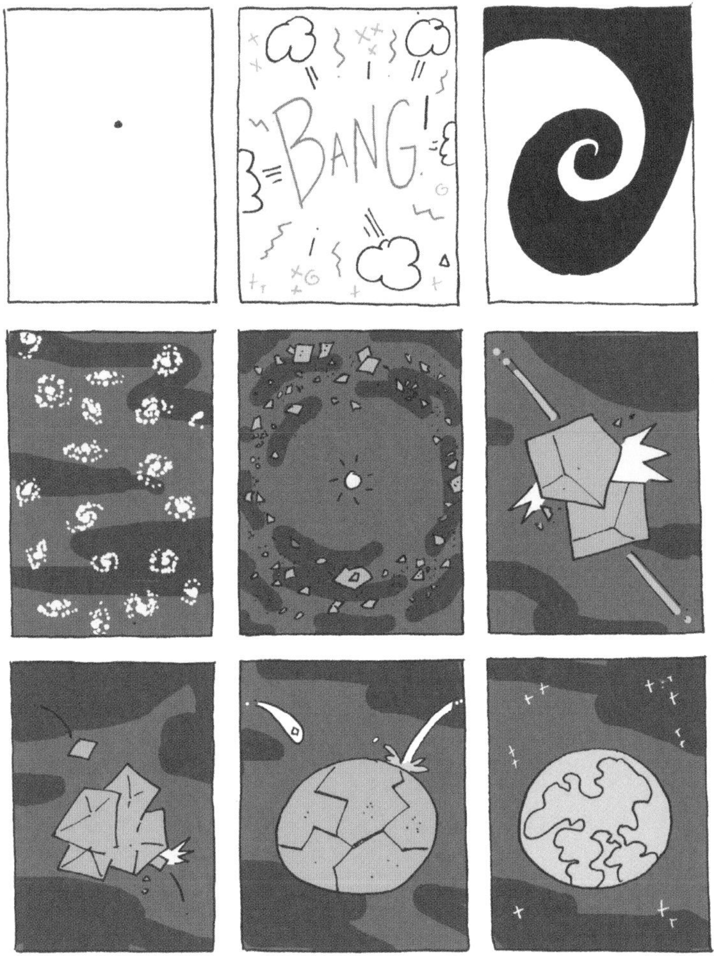
BANG!

BANG

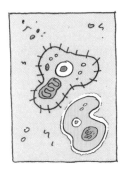

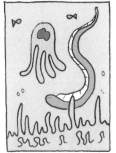

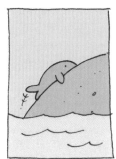

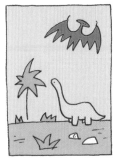

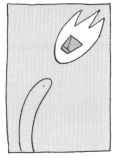

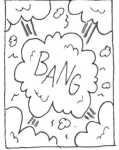

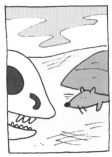

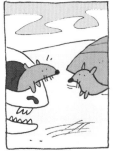

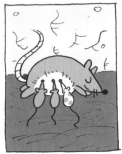

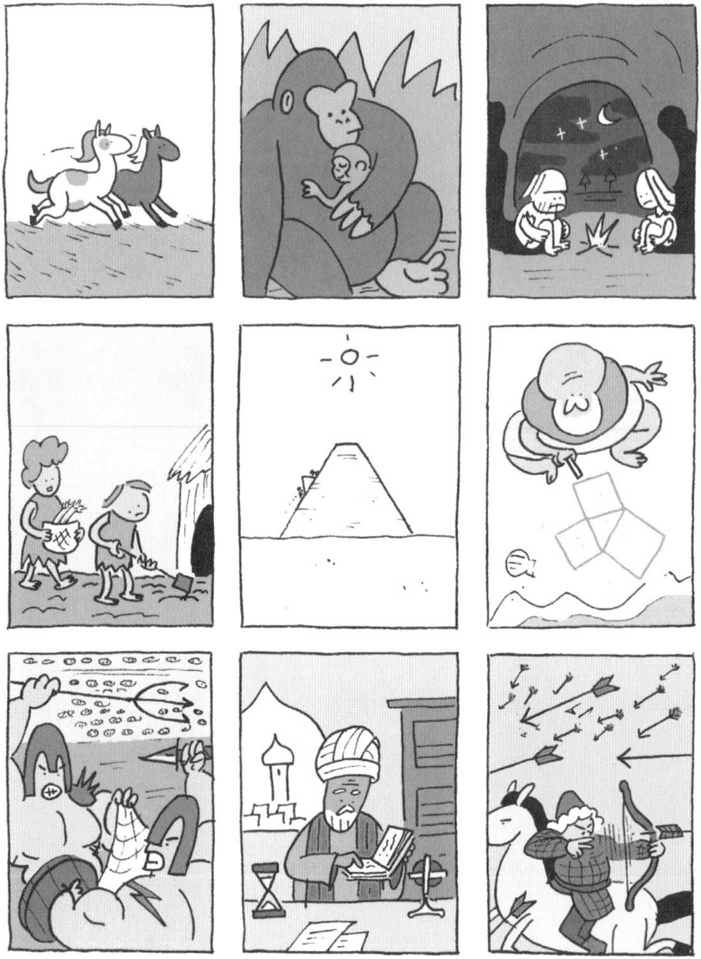

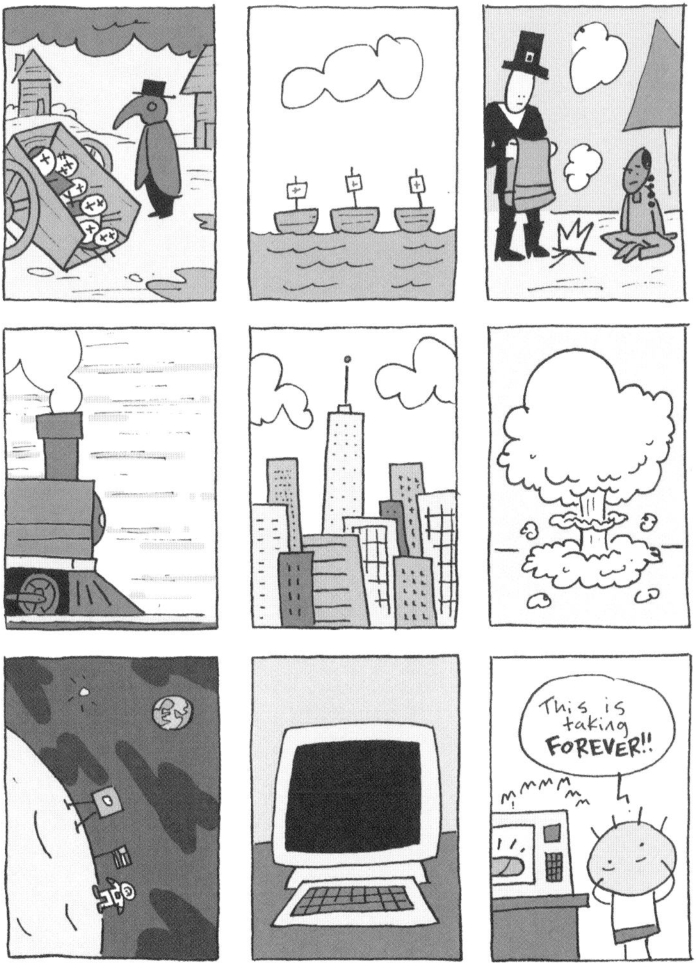

MMMMMM
This is taking FOREVER!!

Certificate of Knowingyness

*This diploma hereby certifies
that the holder has read at least one book
and bestows upon them the privilege
of interrupting any conversation with
"Well, actually..."*

Limit one per customer.

John McNamee, author

The end.

ISBN: 978-1-5493-0306-7

Library of Congress Control Number: 2018956699

10 9 8 7 6 5 4 3 2 1